생활 속의 참선수행 Practice In Daily Life ⑮

The Doctor Is In

내 안에 의사가 있다구요?!

내 안에 의사가 있다구요?!
대행큰스님 법문
생활 속의 참선수행 ⑮ / 한영합본

발행일	2018년 10월 초판1쇄
영문번역	한마음국제문화원
표지디자인	박수연
편집	한마음국제문화원
발행	한마음출판사
출판등록	384-2000-000010
전화	031-470-3175
팩스	031-470-3209
이메일	onemind@hanmaum.org

© 2018 (재)한마음선원
본 출판물은 저작권법에 의하여 보호를 받는 저작물이므로 무단 복제와 무단 전재를 할 수 없습니다.

The Doctor Is In

Practice in Daily Life ⑮ / Bilingual, Korean · English
Dharma Talks by Seon Master Daehaeng

First Edition, First Printing: October 2018
English Translation by
Hanmaum International Culture Institute
Edited by Hanmaum International Culture Institute
Cover Design by Su Yeon Park
Published by Hanmaum Publications
www.hanmaumbooks.org

© 2018 Hanmaum Seonwon Foundation
All rights reserved, including the right to reproduce this work in any form.

Printed in the Republic of Korea

ISBN 978-89-91857-53-7 (04220) / 978-89-91857-50-6 (set)

국립중앙도서관 출판예정도서목록(CIP)

내 안에 의사가 있다구요?! = The doctor is in : 한영합본 / 대행큰스님 법문 ; 영문번역: 한마음국제문화원. -- [안양] : 한마음출판사, 2018
  p. ;   cm. -- (생활 속의 참선수행 =Practice in daily life ; 15)

한영대역본임
ISBN 978-89-91857-53-7 04220 : ₩6000
ISBN 978-89-91857-50-6 (세트) 04220

법문(불경)[法文]
설법[說法]

225.2-KDC6
294.34-DDC23   CIP2018029161

이 도서의 국립중앙도서관 출판예정도서목록(CIP)은 서지정보유통지원시스템 홈페이지(http://seoji.nl.go.kr)와 국가자료공동목록시스템(http://www.nl.go.kr/kolisnet)에서 이용하실 수 있습니다.(CIP제어번호: CIP2018029161)

A CIP catalogue record of the National Library of Korea for this book is available at the homepage of CIP(http://seoji.nl.go.kr) and Korean Library Information System Network(http://www.nl.go.kr/kolisnet). (CIP2018029161)

THE DOCTOR IS IN

Seon Master Daehaeng

내 안에 의사가 있다구요?!

대행큰스님 법문

차 례

10　머리글

12　대행큰스님에 대하여

26　내 안에 의사가 있다구요?!

CONTENTS

11   Foreword

13   About Daehaeng Kun Sunim

27   The Doctor is In

하나로 흐르네

억만 분들이 각을 이루어도

끝없는 한 도량의 한 부처님이시라

한마음 부처님은 말씀하신다

한마음 제 뿌리에 제 나무의 과일 무르익어

이름없는 만 가지의 맛을 내면

세계 평화 이루고

일체 중생 마음의 병 고치니라

-대행큰스님 게송 중에서

Flowing as One

Even though a hundred million people attain enlightenment,

they are all still one Buddha

they are all here in this infinite place of practice.

So says the Buddha of One Mind.

If through this one mind,

our own root,

we cause our own tree to send forth flowers and then bear fruit,

if, through this one mind,

we bring this fruit to ripeness,

this fruit of ten thousand inexpressible flavors,

then this fruit will bring peace to the world,

and heal the illnesses of all sentient beings.

– Daehaeng Kun Sunim

머리글

대행큰스님이 지난 50여 년 동안 끊임없이 중생들에게 베풀어 주신 수많은 법문이 있었지만, 핵심을 짚어 내는 하나의 단어가 있다면, 그건 아마도 "참나"일 것입니다. 항상 나와 함께 있어서 보지 못하는 내 안의 진짜 나, 그 "참나"를 발견하여 당당하고 싱그럽게 살아가기를 바라는, 중생을 위한 스님의 간절한 바람은 이 한 편의 법문 속에도 여지없이 드러나 있습니다.

누구에게나 내면에는 만물만생을 다 먹여 살리고도 되남는 마음속 한 점의 불씨가 있습니다. 그 영원한 불씨를 찾아 광대무변한 마음법의 이치를 체득하여, 진정한 자유인으로서, 우주의 한 일원으로서 당당히 그 역할을 해 나가길 바라는 대행큰스님의 간곡한 뜻이 이 법문을 통해 여러분 모두의 마음에 전해지길 바랍니다.

한마음국제문화원 일동 합장

Foreword

Over the last fifty years, Daehaeng Kun Sunim gave countless Dharma talks and teachings to beings without number, but if all those talks could be summed up into one word, it would be "true self."

This true essence has always been with us, yet remains unseen. Discover it for yourself, and in doing so, learn to live with courage, dignity, and joy. That all beings should awaken to this true essence is Daehaeng Kun Sunim's deepest wish. When you've tasted the most refreshing spring water imaginable, you naturally want to share it with others.

Within us all is this seed, this spark that feeds and sustains each and every being. Discover this eternal spark and realize its profound and unlimited ability. If you can do this, you'll know what it means to truly be a free person, and you can fulfill the great role that is yours as a member of the whole universe.

With palms together,
The Hanmaum International Culture Institute

대행큰스님에 대하여

대행큰스님께서는 여러 면에서 매우 보기 드문 선사(禪師)셨다. 무엇보다 선사라면 당연히 비구 스님을 떠올리는 전통 속에서 여성으로서 선사가 되셨으며, 비구 스님들을 제자로 두었던 유일한 비구니 스님이셨고, 노년층 여성이 주된 신도계층을 이루었던 한국 불교에 젊은 세대의 청장년층 남녀들을 대거 참여하게 만들어 한국불교에 새로운 풍격(風格)을 일으키는 데 일조한 큰 스승이셨다. 또한 전통 비구니 강원과 비구니 종단에 대한 지속적인 지원을 펼치심으로써 비구니 승단을 발전시키는 데 중추적인 역할을 하셨다.

큰스님께서는 어느 누구나 마음수행을 통해 깨달을 수 있음을 강조하시면서 삭발제자와 유발제자를 가리지 않고 법을 구하는 이들에게는 모두 똑같이 가르침을 주셨다.

About Daehaeng Kun Sunim

Daehaeng *Kun Sunim*[1] (1927 − 2012) was a rare teacher in Korea: a female *Seon*(Zen)[2] master, a nun whose students also included monks, and a teacher who helped revitalize Korean Buddhism by dramatically increasing the participation of young people and men.

She broke out of traditional models of spiritual practice to teach in such a way that allowed anyone to practice and awaken, making laypeople a particular focus of her efforts. At

---

1. Sunim / Kun Sunim: Sunim is the respectful title of address for a Buddhist monk or nun in Korea, and Kun Sunim is the title given to outstanding nuns or monks.

2. Seon(禪)(Chan, Zen)**:** Seon describes the unshakeable state where one has firm faith in their inherent foundation, their Buddha-nature, and so returns everything they encounter back to this fundamental mind. It also means letting go of "I," "me," and "mine" throughout one's daily life.

스님은 1927년 서울에서 태어나 일찍이 9세경에 자성을 밝히셨고 당신이 증득(證得)하신 바를 완성하기 위해 오랫동안 산중에서 수행하셨다. 훗날, 누더기가 다 된 해진 옷을 걸치고 손에 주어지는 것만을 먹으며 지냈던 그 당시를 회상하며 스님은 의도적으로 고행을 하고자 했던 것이 아니라 당신에게 주어진 환경이 그러했노라고, 또한 근본 불성자리에 일체를 맡기고 그 맡긴 일이 어떻게 작용하는지를 관하는 일에 완전히 몰두하고 있었기에 다른 것에는 신경을 쓸 틈이 없었노라고 말씀하셨다.

그 시절의 체험이 스님의 가르치는 방식을 형성하는 데 깊은 영향을 미쳤다. 스님은 우리가 본래부터 어마어마한 잠재력을, 무궁무진한 에너지와 지혜를 가지고 있는데도 대부분이 그 역량을 알지 못해 끊임없이 많은 고통을 겪으며 살고 있음을 절실히 느끼며 안타까워하셨다. 우리들 각자 안에 존재하는 이 위대한 빛을 명백히 알고 있었기에, 스님은 본래부터 가지고 있는 근본자성(自性)인 '참나'를 믿고 의지해 살라 가르치셨고, 이 중요한 진리에서 벗어나는 그 어떤 것도 가르치기를 단호히 거부하셨다.

the same time, she was a major force for the advancement of *Bhikkunis*,[3] heavily supporting traditional nuns' colleges as well as the modern Bhikkuni Council of Korea.

Born in Seoul, Korea, she awakened when she was around eight years old and spent the years that followed learning to put her understanding into practice. For years, she wandered the mountains of Korea, wearing ragged clothes and eating only what was at hand. Later, she explained that she hadn't been pursuing some type of asceticism; rather, she was just completely absorbed in entrusting everything to her fundamental *Buddha*[4] essence and observing how that affected her life.

---

3. Bhikkunis: Female sunims who are fully ordained are called *Bhikkuni*(比丘尼) sunims, while male sunims who are fully ordained are called *Bhikku*(比丘) sunims. This can also be a polite way of indicating male or female sunims.

4. Buddha: In this text, "Buddha" is capitalized out of respect, because it represents the essence and function of the enlightened mind. "The Buddha" always refers to Sakyamuni Buddha.

의도한 바는 아니셨지만, 스님은 매일매일의 일상 속에서 누구나 내면에 갖추어 가지고 있는 근본이자 진수(眞髓)인 참나와 진정으로 통할 수 있게 되었을 때 어떠한 일이 일어나는지를 역력히 보여주셨다. 사람들은 스님 곁에 있을 때 자신들을 무한히 받아 주고 품어 주는 것만 같은, 말로 형언키 어려운 정밀(靜謐)한 기운을 느꼈고, 스님이 다른 사람들을 도와줄 때 드러내 보이는 깊은 법력 또한 목도하곤 하였다. 하지만 이 모든 일들은 당신 자신을 돋보이게 하거나 과시하려 했던 게 아니었다. 사실 스님께서는 당신의 법력을 늘 감추려고 하셨다. 마음공부의 목적이 놀라운 능력을 갖게 되는 것이 아님에도 대중들이 그것에만 집착하게 되는 폐단을 우려하셨기 때문이었다.

그렇지만 당신이 하신 모든 일을 통해, 우리가 내면에 있는 근본과 진정으로 하나가 되었을 때 그 능력과 자유로움이 어떤 것인지를 보여주셨다. 스님은 우리 모두가 근본을 통해 연결되어 있으므로 다 통할 수 있고, 그럼으로써 서로 깊이 이해할 수 있다는 것을 보여 주셨으며, 더 나아가 우리가 근본

Those years profoundly shaped Kun Sunim's later teaching style; she intimately knew the great potential, energy, and wisdom inherent within each of us, and recognized that most of the people she encountered suffered because they didn't realize this about themselves. Seeing clearly the great light in every individual, she taught people to rely upon this inherent foundation, and refused to teach anything that distracted from this most important truth.

Without any particular intention to do so, Daehaeng Kun Sunim demonstrated on a daily basis the freedom and ability that arise when we truly connect with this fundamental essence inherent within us.

The sense of acceptance and connection people felt from being around her, as well as the abilities she manifested, weren't things she was trying to show off. In fact, she usually tried to hide them because people would tend to cling to these, without realizing that chasing after them cannot lead to either freedom or awakening.

자리에서 일으키는 한생각이 이 세상에 법이 되어 돌아갈 수 있다는 것도 보여 주셨다.

어떤 의미에서는 이 모든 일이 우리가 만물만생과 정말로 하나가 되었을 때 자연스레 부수적으로 나오는 것이라고 할 수 있다. 상대를 둘로 보거나 방해물로 여기는 마음이 사라졌을 때, 진정으로 모두와 조화롭게 흘러갈 수 있게 되었을 때 이 모든 일이 가능할 수 있게 되는 것이다. 이렇게 되면, 다가오는 상대가 누구든 별개의 존재로 느끼지 않게 된다. 그들이 또 다른 우리 자신들의 모습이기 때문이다. 일체가 둘이 아님을 뼛속 깊이 느끼는 사람이, 어찌 자신 앞에 닥친 인연을 나 몰라라 하고 등져 버릴 수 있겠는가?

스님은 중생들이 가지고 오는 어려운 문제나 상황들을 해결할 수 있도록 도와 주셨으며, 이러한 스님의 자비로운 원력은 당신이 도시로 나와 본격적으로 대중들을 가르치기 이전에 이미 한국에서는 전설이 되어 있었다. 1950년대 말경, 치악산 상원사 근처 한 움막에서 수행차 몇 년간 머무르신 적이 있었는데, 그 소문을 듣고 전국에서 찾아오는 사람들

Nonetheless, in her very life, in everything she did, she was an example of the true freedom and wisdom that arise from this very basic, fundamental essence that we all have – that we are. She showed that because we are all interconnected, we can deeply understand what's going on with others, and that the intentions we give rise to can manifest and function in the world.

All of these are in a sense side effects, things that arise naturally when we are truly one with everyone and everything around us. They happen because we are able to flow in harmony with our world, with no dualistic views or attachments to get in the way. At this point, other beings are not cut off from us; they are another aspect of ourselves. Who, feeling this to their very bones, could turn their back on others?

It was this deep compassion that made her a legend in Korea long before she formally started teaching. She was known for having the spiritual power to help people in all circumstances and with every kind of problem. She compared compassion to freeing a fish from a drying

이 끊이질 않았다. 차마 그들의 고통스런 호소를 내칠 수가 없었던 스님은 일일이 그들의 말에 귀기울이며 마음을 다해 그들을 도와 주셨다. 스님은 자비를 물 마른 웅덩이에서 죽어 가는 물고기를 살리는 방생에 비유하셨다. 집세가 없어 셋집에서 쫓겨난 사람들에게 집을 마련해 주고, 학비가 없어서 학교를 마칠 수 없는 학생들에게 학비를 대주셨지만, 스님의 자비행(慈悲行)을 아는 사람은 손에 꼽을 정도밖에 되지 않았다.

그러나 문제를 해결해 주면 그때뿐 또 다른 문제가 닥쳐오면 속수무책이 되어 버리고 마는 사람들을 보며, 스님께서는 중생들이 자신의 문제를 스스로 해결하고 윤회(輪廻)[1]의 굴레에서 벗어나 자유인이 될 수 있는 도리를 가르치는 일이 더 시급함을 느끼셨다. 누구나가 다 가지고 있는 '참나', 이 내면의 밝디밝은 진수(眞髓)를 알게 하여, 자신들이 자

---

1. 윤회(輪廻): 산스크리트의 삼사라(samsara)를 번역한 말로 쉼 없이 돈다는 생사의 바퀴를 뜻함. 다시 말해, 수레바퀴가 끊임없이 구르는 것과 같이, 중생이 번뇌와 업에 의하여 삼계(三界: 색계, 욕계, 무색계) 육도(六道: 지옥, 아귀, 축생, 아수라, 인간, 천상)라는 생사의 세계를 그치지 않고 돌고 도는 현상을 일컬음.

puddle, putting a homeless family into a home, or providing the school fees that would allow a student to finish high school. And when she did things like this, and more, few knew that she was behind it.

Her compassion was also unconditional. She would offer what help she could to individuals and organizations, whether they be Christian or Buddhist, a private organization or governmental. She would help nun's temples that had no relationship with her temple, Christian organizations that looked after children living on their own, city-run projects to help care for the elderly, and much, much more. Yet, even when she provided material support, always there was the deep, unseen aid she offered through this connection we all share.

However, she saw that ultimately, for people to live freely and go forward in the world as a blessing to all around them, they needed to know about this bright essence that is within each of us.

유롭게 사는 것은 물론이요, 자신들의 삶이 인연 맺은 모든 이에게 축복이 되어 이 한세상을 활달히 살아갈 수 있도록 해야겠다고 다짐하셨다.

마침내 산에서 내려온 스님께서는 1972년 경기도 안양에 한마음선원을 설립하셨다. 이후 40여 년 동안 한마음선원에 주석하시며, 지혜를 원하는 자에게 지혜를, 배고프고 가난한 자에게는 먹을 것과 물질을, 아파하는 자에게는 치유의 방편을 내어 주시는 무한량의 자비를 베푸시며 불법의 진리를 가르쳐 주셨다. 스님은 도움이 필요한 다양한 사회복지 프로그램을 후원하셨고, 6개국에 10개의 국외 지원과 국내 15개의 지원을 세우셨다. 또한 스님의 가르침은 영어, 독어, 스페인어, 러시아어, 중국어, 일본어, 불어, 이태리어, 베트남어, 체코어, 인도네시아어 등으로 번역 출간되었다. 스님은 2012년 5월 22일 0시, 세납 86세로 입적하셨으며, 법랍 63세셨다.

To help people discover this for themselves, she founded the first *Hanmaum*[5] Seon Center in 1972. For the next forty years she gave wisdom to those who needed wisdom, food and money to those who were poor and hungry, and compassion to those who were hurting.

---

5. Hanmaum[han-ma-um]: *Han* means one, great, and combined, while *maum* means mind, as well as heart, and together they mean everything combined and connected as one.

What is called *Hanmaum* is intangible, unseen, and transcends time and space. It has no beginning or end, and is sometimes called our fundamental mind. It also means the mind of all beings and everything in the universe connected and working together as one. In English, we usually translate this as *one mind*.

본 저서는 대행큰스님의 법문을
한국어와 영어 합본 시리즈로 출간하는
〈생활 속의 참선수행〉시리즈 제15권으로
1992년 12월 20일 정기법회 때 설하신 내용을
재편집한 것입니다. 몇 개의 질문은 다른 법문에서
발췌해 추가하였습니다.

This Dharma talk was given by
Daehaeng Kun Sunim on Sunday, Dec. 20, 1992,
with some related questions added from other talks.
This is Volume 15 in the ongoing series,
Practice in Daily Life.

Daehaeng Kun Sunim founded ten overseas branches of Hanmaum Seon Center, and her teachings have been translated into twelve different languages to date: English, German, Russian, Chinese, French, Spanish, Indonesian, Italian, Japanese, Vietnamese, Estonian, and Czech, in addition to the original Korean. For more information about these or the overseas centers, please see the back of this book.

내 안에 의사가 있다구요?!

1992년 12월 20일

여러 지원에서 온 신도님들과 본원의 신도님들이 다 같이 한자리를 하게 돼서 더욱더 반갑습니다. 언제는 뭐, 아니었습니까마는 오늘 뵙고 보니 특별히 더 반갑습니다. (합장하시며) 대구 합창단분들도 오셨군요.

우리 속담에 뭉치면 살고 흩어지면 죽는다는 말이 있죠. 미생물도 인간의 생명도 지·수·화·풍(地水火風)이 한데 뭉쳤기 때문에 생기는 거고 죽으면 흩어집니다. 인간이 하나 나오려면 양 부모의 뜻과 내 영혼의 뜻이 만나야 하며, 그렇게 만나면 악하든 선하든 자기가 지은 업식(業識)[2]이 한데 합쳐

---

2. 업식(業識): 과거 생(生)에 지은 모든 행위와 생각이 현재 우리의 몸속에 있는 생명들의 의식에 그대로 기록되어 잠재되어 있는 것. 때가 되면 이 의식들이 하나씩 풀려 나와 여러 가지 형태로 우리들 앞에 펼쳐지게 됨. 이러한 의식들을 녹이는 방법은 발생하는 모든 문제를 자신의 근본자리에 지속적으로 맡기는 것이며, 업식도 원래는 공(空)한 것이니, 업식이 있다는 생각 자체에 착을 두지 않아야 함.

The Doctor is In

December 20, 1992

It's always nice to be here together with you, and today seems particularly wonderful because so many people have come here from the branch temples. [Putting her hands together and bowing.] I see that we even have the choir from Daegu here as well!

You all know the Korean proverb, "Stick together and live. Scatter and die," right? Well, microbes as well as human beings are functioning like this. They all come into existence because earth, water, fire, and air gather together like this. In order for that to happen, there first has to be an affinity between both parents as well as ourselves. Once that connects, all of our *karmic consciousnesses*,[6] both good and bad, gather together and then form a body, with which we can be born into this world.

져 이 세상에 형성돼 나오게 됩니다. 이 모든 것이 지·수·화·풍으로 흩어져 있다 뭉쳤다 하는 겁니다. 그래서 이 지·수·화·풍이 아니라면 인간이 태어날 수도 없고, 또 이렇게 소통하면서 최고의 동물로서의 활동도 못할 겁니다.

지금 세계적으로 이 지·수·화·풍을 바탕으로 한 연구들이 많습니다. 그런데 기본적으로 내가 지·수·화·풍을 바탕으로 형성됐으나, 그러한 나의 주인이 내 마음[3]이니 이 마음을 떠나서는 근원적인 연구를 할 수가 없습니다. 과학자들 중에는 이것을 무의식적으로라도 아는 사람들이 있습니다. 그러니까 마음을 통해 두뇌로 해서 연구가 이루어지기도 하는 거겠죠.

---

3. 마음: 단순히 두뇌를 통한 정신활동이나 지성을 일컫는 말이 아니라, 만물만생이 지니고 있으며, 일체만법을 움직이게 하는 천지의 근본을 뜻함. '안에 있다, 밖에 있다' 혹은, '이거다 저거다'라고 말할 수 없으며 시작과 끝이 없고 사라질 수도 파괴될 수도 없음. 시공을 초월하여 존재함.

All of this is possible because of the gathering and scattering of the four elements. We could not have been born as human beings, nor could we communicate as we do, nor could we fulfill our role as the highest animal without the gathering and scattering of the four elements. Likewise, they form the basis of much of science and scientific research.

Our physical aspect is all based on the four elements, but what organizes and directs all this is our *fundamental mind*,[7] our Buddha-nature. Thus any kind of research or exploration has to include this fundamental mind; it has to be carried out at

---

6. Karmic consciousness: Our thoughts, feelings, and behaviors are recorded as the consciousnesses of the lives that make up our body. These are sometimes called karmic consciousnesses, although they don't have independent awareness or volition. Sometime afterwards, these consciousnesses will come back out.

Thus, we may feel happy, sad, angry, etc., without an obvious reason, or they may cause other problems to occur. The way to dissolve these consciousnesses is not to react to them when they arise, but instead to entrust them to our foundation. However, even these consciousnesses are just temporary combinations, so we shouldn't cling to the concept of them.

어쨌든 이런 연구들을 통해 지금 생활 속에 없어서는 안 되는 새로운 것들이 개발되는 겁니다. 지·수·화·풍을 바탕으로 생각을 발전시켰으니 고체, 액체, 기체란 말을 붙여 구분 지어 연구도 하고, 나아가 레이저 광선 같은 것도 개발이 된 겁니다.

이름도 용도에 맞게 참 잘 지었어요. 그 레이저 광선을 지금 우리가 여기저기에 얼마나 긴요히 잘 쓰고 있습니까? 특히 병원에서요. 이런 종류의 기술들은 비행기, 인공위성, 라디오, TV, 전화 할 것 없이 너무 다양하게 쓰여서 지금은 없어선 안 되는 존재예요. 어디서나 쓰이죠. 멀리도 갈 수 있고 물론 가깝게도 갈 수 있고, 과거엔 할 수 없었던 많은 것들을 다 할 수 있게 합니다.

least in part through this fundamental mind. Many scientists and researchers already understand this, if only half-consciously. They use their intellect and knowledge, of course, but they also put that to work through their fundamental mind.

In this way they've been able to create all kinds of new materials and technology that we now find indispensable. Starting with earth, water, fire, and air, scientists developed the ideas and theories that led to further developments, like lasers and such.

"Laser," somebody sure came up with a good name. Those are used everywhere, aren't they? In hospitals, planes, satellites, radio, TV, phones – lasers have become indispensable in our lives. They can be used across vast distances, as well as very close distances.

---

7. Fundamental mind: This refers to our inherent essence, that which we fundamentally are. "Mind," in Mahayana Buddhism, almost never means the brain or intellect. Instead it refers to the essence through which we are connected to everything, everywhere. It is intangible, beyond space and time, and has no beginning or end. It is the source of everything, and everyone is endowed with it. "Fundamental mind" is interchangeable with other terms such as "Buddha-nature," "true nature," "true self," and "foundation."

The Doctor is In

이렇게 첨단의 기술은 굉장한 거예요. 하지만 우리가 하는 이 마음공부와 한번 비교해 보십시오. 과거로 돌아갔다가 올 수도 있고, 미래로 갔다가 올 수도 있고 또 어떠한 업식이라도 녹일 수 있습니다. 말하자면 윤회성이나 유전성, 영계성, 세균성, 업보성 이런 것들로 오는 모두를 녹여 달라지게 할 수 있는 겁니다. 그뿐이 아닙니다. 만 명이 있다 하더라도 내가 그 만 명이 될 수 있고 그 만 명이 내가 될 수 있는 공부입니다. 여기에서 만이라고 하는 숫자는 의미가 없습니다. 석가모니 부처님께서는 어떤 거든지 나투어서 응신[4]이 되어 내가 되지 않는 것이 없다고 했습니다. 너, 나가 둘이 아니게 되는 겁니다.

---

4. 응신(應身): 법신(法身)이 다양한 중생들을 구제하기 위하여 응해주고 둘이 아니게 모습을 나투어 보살행을 하는 것.

Although all of their uses are amazing, let's look at what's possible through spiritual practice and *relying upon our fundamental mind*.[8] We can go to the past and return, we can go to the future, and any kind of karma can be melted down.

---

8. Relying upon our fundamental mind: Trusting and relying upon our fundamental mind is the essence of spiritual practice and growth in all Daehaeng Kun Sunim's teachings. It's the foundation of all spiritual progress. We all have this Buddha-nature, this original face, this inherent mind, and, In fact, everything in our life revolves around it.

When teaching people about spiritual practice, Daehaeng Kun Sunim always emphasized that the very first step was just being aware that we all have this inherent nature. The next step was trying to rely upon it. This means taking what's confronting us, what's arising in our life, and doing our best to entrust that to this fundamental essence and then to let go of it. As we entrust something, we let go of it and just be aware, observing what's going on, without trying to watch too closely and see what happens.

As we keep working at this, we'll get experiences, times when everything seems to just click into place. We will experience times when we truly let go unconditionally, without a lot of "I" or "me," letting this inherent Buddha-nature take care of what we entrusted. As we see it working, as we experience this for ourselves, our faith in it naturally becomes deeper, and we are better able to entrust more and more. This practice of relying upon our fundamental mind, our Buddha-nature, is a self-correcting path that seems narrow in the beginning, but which eventually becomes a great highway.

The Doctor is In

다시 말해 이 공부는 시간을 초월해 자유자재(自由自在)할 수도 있거니와, 과거에 어떻게 살았느냐에 따라 찰나찰나 지금 생활 속에서 나오는 모든 업보 그 자체를 녹여 미래를 바꿀 수 있는 겁니다.

또한 가깝든지 멀든지 그걸 불문에 부치고, 끌어다 보려면 끌어다 보고, 놓고 보려면 놓고 보고, 갖다 먹을 수 있으면 갖다 먹고, 갖다 줄 수 있으면 갖다 주고, 자유자재로 할 수 있게 하는 그런 공부입니다.

Problems caused by *samsara*,[9] genetics, ghosts, germs, and karma can all be dissolved and changed into something positive. Not only this. If, for example, there are ten thousand people, then through this practice, you can become those ten thousand people, and they can become you. In the face of this practice, numbers have no meaning. Buddha can become one with anything, and manifest and respond to it all. In the midst of this, how could there be any separation between you and me?

Through knowing and relying upon our foundation we can be utterly free of all hindrances, have the ability to help with whatever is needed, be able to transcend time, and able to finally dissolve all of our old karma as it continuously comes out in our lives. In so doing we can even change our future.

Regardless of whether something is near or far, if you want to see it, then you'll see it as if it was brought before you. If you want to examine it, then

---

9. Samsara: The endless cycle of birth and death that all living things are continuously passing through.

날아가는 새도 떨어뜨릴 수 있는 공부입니다. 로켓도 올라가는 걸 멈추게 하려면 멈추고 없애려면 없앨 수 있는 공부입니다. 이건 엄청난 공부입니다. 말로 어떻게 다 하겠습니까? 이 공부를 하면 자유대권을 갖는데. 이 천지, 우주 천지의 모든 대권의 소유자인데 뭘 더 얘기하겠습니까?

하지만 이렇게 대단한 것이라 말을 해 준다고 아무나 이해할 수 있는 게 아니기에 석가모니 부처님께서도 근기에 따라 말씀을 하셨습니다. 요만큼 가지고 있는 사람에게는 요만큼 얘기를 하시고, 이만큼 가진 사람에게는 이만큼 얘기를 하셨습니다. 왜냐하면 아무리 줘도 흘러버리기 때문입니다.

you'll see it down to the smallest aspect. If you need something, you'll be able to bring it forth and use it, and if something is needed elsewhere, you'll be able to bring that forth too and give it. Through this practice, you do all of this freely, as needed.

If you want the birds of the air to land on the ground, then they will, and if you want to stop a missile from flying up into the sky, this too will happen. Knowing and connecting with this foundation of ours is just so incredible – how can I describe it all? The ability and authority that this practice bestows is inconceivable. It's like being given the authority to take care of anything in the *universe*.[10]

Even here, I'm only talking about just the things that people can easily understand and follow. Sakyamuni Buddha too, taught people according to their ability to understand. To those of great capacity, he taught much. To those of more limited capacity, he taught only a little, in a way that they

---

10. Universe: This includes all visible realms, as well as all unseen realms.

또한 이 공부는 말로, 지식으로, 학식으로 해서 알아지는 게 아닙니다. 남녀노소 귀천이 없이 누구나 스스로 마음공부[5]를 통해 알아지는 겁니다. 부처님 당시에 유마힐(維摩詰)[6] 거사와 석가모니 부처님이 도반(道伴)[7]이 되셨는데 어느 누구라도 이런 공부를 할 수 있다는 것을 방편(方便)으로 보여 주신 거지요.

---

5. 마음공부: 진정한 자유인이 되기 위해 자신의 마음이 어떻게 작용하고 변하는지를 관찰하고 배우며, 그것을 실제 생활 속에서 응용하고 체험해 보면서 알아가는 모든 과정을 뜻함.

6. 유마힐(維摩詰, *Vimalakirti*): 유마힐은 산스크리트 *Vimalakirti*의 음역으로써 '깨끗한 이름(淨名)' 또는 '때묻지 않는 이름(無垢稱)'이라는 뜻을 가지고 있음. 인도 중부지방에 위치한 바이샤리의 부호(富豪)로서 석가모니 부처님과 동시대인으로 여겨짐. 불법의 진수를 체득하고 청정한 행위를 실천하며 가난한 자에게는 도움을 주고 불량한 자에게는 훈계를 주어 올바른 가르침을 전하고자 노력하여 세속에 있으면서도 불도를 실천하고 완성한 재가신자(在家信者)의 이상상(理想像)으로 알려져 있음.

7. 도반(道伴): 함께 도(道)를 닦는 벗.

could understand. Because that was all they could absorb.

For this is something that can only be learned through practice, right where we are. Other people's words, theories, or intellectual learning can't take the place of our own experience and knowledge. Old, young, male, female, noble, lowly, whoever, we can only truly understand the essence of what the Buddha spoke of through this practice of relying upon our fundamental mind.

When Sakyamuni declared that the layman *Vimalakirti*[11] was his own *Dharma brother*,[12] it was to make it clear that this practice was available to anyone and everyone.

---

11. Vimalakirti: A lay disciple of Sakyamuni Buddha who was renowned for the depth of his enlightenment. His name means "Pure" or "Unstained." He appears in the Vimalakirti-Nirdesa Sutra, where he taught even the great disciples of the Buddha. He is portrayed as the ideal layperson, one who attained the essence of the Buddha-dharma and who thoroughly applied his understanding to his life. He would help those who were poor and suffering, and teach and educate those who were behaving badly.

12. Dharma brother: A fellow practitioner. There is also a strong nuance of recognition of Vimalakirti as someone of impressive spiritual depth and standing.

가만히 생각을 해 보십시오. 우리가 지구에서 이렇게 살아가는 동물로서 어떤 때 생각을 하면 모두가 하찮게 생각이 되면서도, 한편으론 생명의 존엄성을 알고 그걸 지키려고 합니다.

미생물에서부터 인간까지 모두가 먹고 먹히는 아픔을 껴안고 전쟁 아닌 전쟁을 합니다. 얼마나 치열합니까? 칼을 들어야만이 싸움이 아닙니다. 이런 뼈저린 아픔을 견디면서 우리가 지금껏 왔으니 이제는 세상 돌아가는 걸 좁게만 보지 마시고 한번 넓게 펼쳐서 봐 보십시오. 어떠한가?

누가 뒤에서 쫓아와서 쫓기는 게 아닌데도 쫓기고 있고, 잡아먹으려고 쫓다가도 잡아 먹히는 그런 세상을 우리 모두 살고 있습니다. 태어날 때부터 장애를 갖고 나오는 경우도 있고, 육신이 널성하게 살다가도 어느 순간에 자기한테 왜 그런 일이 생기는지도 모르는 채 장애자가 되는 일이 벌어지기도 합니다. 정신장애도 마찬가지입니다. 어떻게 생각하면 사는 게 쓸데없다는 생각이 들기도 할 때가 있죠. 기가 막혀 하늘을 쳐다보고 웃은 적이 한두 번이 아닙니다.

Please think about this. From the perspective of the Earth, human beings are just another animal, and often act no better than animals. Nonetheless, they have a sense of the preciousness of all life, and often work to protect it all.

Yet from microbes all the way to humans, everyone has been killing and eating each other, or being killed and eaten. It seems like just endless pain and war on an unimaginable scale. It's so vicious. Battles are happening all the time where neither sword nor gun is drawn. Now, having made it through all of this pain and suffering, stop acting like someone stuck in those lower levels! Right here, start seeing the world from a higher, broader perspective. See how things look.

People are being chased, even though no one is chasing them, and are being hunted and eaten, even as they hunt and eat others. This is the world we are living in. You may be completely healthy, yet suddenly become disabled without even knowing why. Or you could be suddenly struck down by a mental disability. Sometimes, seeing people go through this again and again, without ever trying to escape from it, gets too much for me, and I can only look at the heavens and sigh.

세상이 이렇게 서로 연결되어 얽혀 돌아가는데도 그 이치를 모르고 내 몸, 내 가정만 생각하며 모든 걸 아주 좁게 살아가니까 한 치 앞을 내다볼 수 없는 거지요.

그러니 더 막막하단 말입니다. 그런 걸 보고 있자면 어떤 땐 너무 안타까워 '그저 나 같은 바보만이라도 되면 먹고 먹히는 이런 항아리 속에서 쫓고 쫓기지는 않을 텐데…'라는 생각을 하기도 합니다.

불교라 하면 사찰에 다니면서 그저 불상에 절하고 부처님 믿는 거로 생각들 하시지만 그게 아닙니다. 석가모니 부처님께서는 "너부터 알라." 하고 명확히 말씀하셨습니다. 또 "네 몸뚱이가 내 몸뚱이하고 다른 게 있느냐? 네 마음이나 내 마음이나 다른 게 있느냐? 육신도 마음도 다른 게 없다. 그런데 생각의 차이가 있다."라고도 하셨습니다.

Everything in the world is connected and tied together, but people don't know this, and instead put all their focus on "my body," "my family." They don't learn to see the larger context, and end up unable to see what's coming towards them, even when it's only an inch away.

Not seeing any farther, they don't know what they should truly be doing, nor how to find a way forward. What I see what people go through… [Sighs.] If they'd just throw everything away, and keep doing that, then even though they lived like some kind of kindly fool, they could stop hunting and killing each other. They wouldn't be chasing and biting each other like two rats trapped in a bucket.

Sometimes people think that Buddhism is going to the temple and expecting that the Buddha will save them, but that's not it. Sakyamuni Buddha told everyone very clearly "Know yourself." He said to them, "Do you think my body is any different from yours? Do you really think that my mind is any different? Both are exactly the same as yours. The only difference is in the kinds of thoughts I give rise to."

전 세계적으로 기독교니 가톨릭교니 이슬람교니 불교니, 곳곳에 종교가 없는 곳이 없고 모두들 자기 나름대로의 믿음을 갖고 있습니다만, 가만히 보면 대부분이 기복이에요. 어쩌면 그렇게, 자기 앞 한 치도 내다보지 못하게 자기 눈을 막아 놓고는 상대만 믿고 가요?

내가 항상 여러분한테 말하지만, 내 근본, 나 자신이 아닌 상대를 믿고 그렇게 가다보면 세세생생 노예밖에 더 되겠습니까? 종노릇밖에 더 하겠습니까?

부처님 가르침은 종노릇하라는 게 아닙니다. "당당하게 너는 땅을 짚고 일어나거라. 절름발이가 되지 말고, 눈뜬장님이 되지 말고, 귀머거리가 되지 말아라. 이 우주 천하 모든 도리천(忉利天)은 너의 마음에 직결되어 있다." 이렇게 가르치셨습니다.

Everywhere you go in the world you'll find some form of religion, won't you? Catholicism, Protestantism, Buddhism, Islam, and they all have their own beliefs and faith. Yet if you look closely at how people are behaving, they are trying to convince some outer power to give them what they want. They obscure their own inner eye, and end up being unable to see even an inch in front of themselves. They are clueless about what's happening to them, and clueless about what's developing in front of them.

If you put all your faith in others, and ignore what you already have within, then for life after life you be no more than a slave. Do you really want to live as a poor sharecropper?

The Buddha did not teach people to become beggars. He taught how to walk the Earth with dignity. Don't be lame, don't be blind, and don't be deaf. Know that all of the universe, all of the great Dharma realms, and all of their power, ability, and energy are directly connected to your mind. This is what he taught!

Whenever the layman Vimalakirti met monks who were focused on sitting meditation, he would

지난번에도 얘기했지만, 유마힐 거사 역시 마찬가지로 스님네들이 앉아서 좌선하고 있는 걸 보면 "좌선을 했다 일어나면 끊어지지 않느냐!" 하고 충고도 하면서 여러 가지로 일러 주셨다 이겁니다.

또 "내 몸이 나으려면 중생들이 다 나아야 내 몸이 낫지 않느냐!"라고도 했는데, 사람들은 그것을 자기 안의 중생인 줄 모르고 바깥 세계의 중생들을 다 거둬야 자기 몸이 낫는 것으로 이렇게 착각을 해요.

내 몸속의 중생들이, 그 생명의 의식들이 작용해서 고쳐 나가야 나도 낫는 거 아닙니까? 각자 여러분 말입니다. 몸속의 그 생명들, 그 의식들이 나와 둘이 아니라는 것을 알고, 내 마음이 그 의식들에게도 우리가 하나라는 걸 알게 해시 질 이끌고 가야 합니다.

ask them, "What happens when you stand up? Doesn't your practice then come to an end? He would counsel them, and teach them like this so that they could find their own way forward.

He also said, "My body will become healthy only after all unenlightened beings become healthy." People often misunderstand this and think that he meant that he had to save all of the beings outside his body in order for his own illness to be healed.

But it's the lives within the body that have to be saved in order for the body to be healed. If their consciousnesses can be raised so that they work together harmoniously, then as those lives begin to function properly, the body as a whole will be healed.

We need to teach those lives within us, those consciousnesses, that they do not exist apart from each other. It's through this fundamental mind of ours that we can teach them that we are all part of the same whole. This is how we have to guide all of the unenlightened beings that make up our body.

내가 항상 얘기했죠, 지구가 어디로 돌아다니는지 우리는 가늠할 수가 없노라고. 이와 마찬가지로 모든 오장육부의 생명들, 생명체는 우리 인간이 부산으로 가는지 서울로 가는지 모릅니다. 그걸 알게 해 줘야죠. 그래야 내가 마음먹는 대로 같이 뭉쳐, 같이 **한마음**[8]을 내서, 들일 건 들이고 낼 건 내며, 자유자재권을 형성시켜 나가야 그것이 천백억 **화신**[9]으로 화(化)하죠.

그러니까 다시 말해 나의 그 모든 수십억의 의식들이 한마음으로 뭉쳐서 필요에 따라 내가 생각하는 대로, 내가 말하는 대로 같이해 줄 수 있는 그런 심력(心力)을 길러야 된다는 얘깁니다.

---

8. 한마음: '한'이란 광대무변함, 일체가 하나로 합쳐진 것을 뜻하며, 한마음이란 만질 수도 없고 보이지도 않으며, 시공간을 초월하여, 시작도 끝도 없는 근본마음을 말함. 또한, 만물만생의 마음이 삼천대천세계와 서로 연결되어 하나로 돌아가는 것을 의미하기도 함. 다시 말해, 한마음은 우주 전체와 그 속에서 살고 있는 일체 생명들이 근본을 통해 서로 연결되어 그 마음들이 하나로 돌아가는 모든 작용을 포함하고 있음.

9. 화신(化神): 모든 것을 자기의 근본자리에 놓았을 때 한생각에 따라 현실로 화(化)하여 드러나는 것.

We, as individuals, have no sense of where the Earth is going, do we? Just like this, the lives that make up our organs, flesh, and bones have no idea if this body is headed towards Busan or Seoul. It's up to us to communicate with them and let them know what's going on. Only then, can all the consciousnesses of the lives within us are fully work together, and respond as one to our intentions. Then we can bring in whatever is needed and send out what needs to be sent out, and function with complete freedom, manifesting in a million different ways, according to the need.

Let me put it this way: You have to be able to get all of these billions of consciousnesses within you to respond to and follow your words and intentions. You do this by gathering them together in your *one mind*,[13] and you keep doing this. You

---

13. One mind (*Hanmaum* [han-ma-um]): From the Korean, where "one" has a nuance of great and combined, while "mind" is more than intellect and includes "heart" as well. Together, they mean everything combined and connected as one. What is called "one mind" is intangible, unseen, and transcends time and space. It has no beginning or end, and is sometimes called our fundamental mind. It also means the mind of all beings and everything in the universe connected and working together as one.

The Doctor is In

그런데 이렇게 끌고 갈 수 있는 내 마음, 내 근본마음이 있다는 걸 모르고 그걸 믿질 못해, 의식들이 의식들대로 놀게 합니다. 내 이 마음을 믿고 모든 걸 일임하지 않으면 위(胃) 공장은 위 공장대로 따로 놀고 장(腸)공장은 장 공장대로 따로 놀고 방광 공장, 척수 공장, 척추 공장, 콩팥 공장, 심장 공장 이 모든 장기가 각각 따로 놀게 되는 겁니다.

호랑이 없는 산에는 여우가 왕이라고 그러죠? 모든 세포, 장기가 다 내가 제일이라고 하거든요. 그러니 하나로 따라 주지 않는 거죠. 그렇게 되면 앞에 닥친 어떠한 일도 대처를 못 합니다.

이 마음이란 것은 색도 없고 형체도 없습니다. 역력하게 무언가가 있어서 볼 수도 있고 쥘 수도 있고 그렇다면, 이 삼천대천세계를 집어삼킬 수도 없고, 자유자재할 수 있는 그러한 대권을 가질 수도 없겠지요. 그런 게 없기 때문에 그렇게 자유자재로 활용할 수 있는 거예요.

have to keep doing this. Then they'll begin to follow your intentions. You have to develop this kind of spiritual ability.

But so many people don't realize that each of us has this fundamental mind, and so they don't try to make it their center, and because there is no center, the consciousnesses of the lives within wander off on their own. If we don't try to rely upon our fundamental mind, this true essence, and entrust it with everything we face, then all the parts of our body will function as if they were isolated from the whole. The stomach would do its own thing, the intestines, the bladder, the spine, the kidneys, and so on, would all act without understanding their part in the whole.

It's like the old saying, "If there's no tiger on the mountain, the foxes run around thinking each is the lord of creation." It's like each part of the body thinks it alone is the boss, and so won't follow any other part. And it won't follow your intentions. How then could you respond when the truly hard parts of life arise?

This mind has no form or color or fixed shape. It embraces the entire universe and all lives within,

보여 주기 위한 뭐, 그런 장난으로 하는 거 말고, 모든 걸 다 따져 봤을 때 내가 이거는 꼭 필요하다 하면 틀림없이 레이저 광선이 쫘 들어가듯이, 아니 그것보다도 더 빨리 한 찰나에 들 수 있습니다.

어쩌면들 그렇게 일러 줘도 상대는 쉽게 믿으면서 자신은 못 믿는지, '옛날의 선지식(善知識)[10]들이 얼마나 답답했을까?' 하는 생각을 합니다. 다들 자기가 그런 영향력을 가지고 있는데도 불구하고 자신들을 믿지 못해요. 그렇게 믿지 못하는데 어떻게 이 우주 천지를 다스리겠습니까?

내가 '다스린다'는 말을 써서 그렇지, 우주 천지를 다스린다고 할 때는 내가 높아서 다스리는 게 아닙니다. 불에 들어가면 불덩어리와 하나가 될 수 있고, 물에 들어가면 물과 하나가 될 수 있고, 허공

---

10. 선지식(善知識): 불법의 진리를 가르쳐 주며, 사람들을 바른 길로 이끌어주는 훌륭한 지도자 혹은 현자(賢者)를 뜻함.

freely functioning and taking care of everything, using power and ability beyond imagining. It can do all of this exactly because it is not some limited, material thing.

When you're looking at all aspects of a thing, and decide what's needed, this mind races forward to take care of it. Faster than even a laser beam. You can use the ability of your mind to take care of anything in the universe, but, frankly, often times people use it only for such small, petty things that it's a bit like children showing off or playing with toys.

Even though I tell people all about how this works, they are still so quick to believe in others, and so reluctant to believe in their own essence. I'll bet this has frustrated everyone who's ever awakened. Even though everyone has this great power within themselves to affect the world around them, they refuse to trust this. They could rule over everything in the universe if they would just trust this ability.

I've used the words, "rule over," didn't I? But when I say "rule over" or "govern the entire universe," I don't mean doing this from some high

에서는 공기와 하나가 되고, 땅에서는 흙과 하나가 될 수 있어야 하며, 보이지 않는 영계로 들어가면 영가(靈駕)와 하나가 되고, 산 사람을 돕고자 한다면 그 사람과 하나가 될 수 있는, 즉 모든 것이 내가 될 수 있어야만이 그런 여건이 주어지는 겁니다.

그런데 따로 떨어져 있는 대상도 아니고, 요 몸뚱이 속에 있는 의식들이 동료로서 나와 하나가 되어 같이 움죽거린다는데 그것도 못 믿으니 어떡합니까? 그것부터 믿어야 되는데 말이에요. 아무리 회초리가 가늘고 보잘것없다 하더라도 한데 합쳐서 이렇게 뭉쳐 놓으면 꺾을 수가 없습니다. 그와 같이 내 몸뚱이 속의 그 수십억 의식들이 따로따로 놓고 보면 미미한 존재들이겠지만 한데 합쳐 돌아가게 하면 이찌, 누가 그걸 꺾겠습니까? 이것부디 아셔야 되지 않을까 생각이 됩니다.

ranking position and forcing everything to do what I want. Instead, I mean that if you meet fire, then you become one with it. When you meet air, you become one with it, and meeting the earth, you become one with it. Encountering unseen spirits of the dead, you become one with them. Meeting living people, you become one with them. Only when you can truly become one with whatever you meet, will you be able to take care of anything that arises.

So then, what of the lives that make up our very own body? Shouldn't we also become one with them? You are completely capable of this. Never doubt that you can become one with all these lives inside you. Even though a single twig seems weak and insignificant, if you gather a bunch of them together into a bundle, they become unbreakable, don't they? Then what of all the billions of lives within our bodies? Although each is tiny and fragile, if they all function together as one, nothing can overcome them. So having faith that you can gather all of these lives together is where you have to start.

여러분 중엔 맡겼는데도 아픈 것이 낫지 않으면 '에이, 주인공[11]도 쓸데없어.' 이렇게 일축해 버리는 분들이 계십니다. 주인공에게 맡겼던 일이 잘 안 풀린다고 '에이그, 이게 무슨….' 하고 쉽게 포기하고 버릴 사람이니까 안 되는 겁니다. 쌓인 업식이 많으니 제대로 맡기는 것도 수월치 않은데다 한두 번 맡긴다고 고통을 주는 그 업식들이 쉽게 사라지는 게 아닌데 말이에요.

예전에 이런 일이 있었지요. 충주에 있는 어느 시멘트 공장에 다니는 사람의 부인인데 백혈병에 걸렸다며 나를 찾아왔습니다. 그런데 아파서 집안일도 잘 못하고 돈도 많이 들어간다며 남편의 구박이 자심(滋甚)해서 왔다고 하더라고요.

---

11. 주인공(主人空): 우리 모두 스스로 갖추어 가지고 있는 근본마음으로 일체 만물만생의 근본과 직결된 자리. 나를 존재하게 하고, 나를 움직이게 하며, 내 모든 것을 관장하는 참 주인이므로 주인(主人)이며, 매 순간 쉴 사이 없이 변하고 돌아가 고정된 실체가 없으므로 비어 있다고 할 수 있기 때문에 빌 공(空)자를 써서, 주인공(主人空)이라 함. 본래면목, 성품, 불성 등 여러 가지로 지칭할 수 있음.

There are some people who turn their back on *Juingong*[14] when they don't immediately get better after trying to entrust their illness. They try for a little bit but then give up. Because they give up so easily, nothing has a chance to develop. But when a problem is being caused by a giant pile of karmic consciousnesses, do you think that just letting go once or twice will be enough?

Let me tell you a story about something that happened a long time ago, when a woman from Chungju visited me in tears. She had been ill for some time and finally came up to Seoul to see a specialist, and who diagnosed her with leukemia. Because she'd been sick, she hadn't been able to do much housework, and had spent a lot of money on doctors, so her husband was giving her a hard time.

---

14. Juingong (主人空, [Ju-in-gong]): Pronounced "ju-in-gong." *Juin*(主人) means the true doer or the master, and *gong*(空) means empty. Thus, Juingong is our true nature, our true essence, the master within that is always changing and manifesting, with no fixed form or shape.

Daehaeng Sunim has compared Juingong to the root of the tree. Our bodies and consciousness are like the branches and leaves, but it is the root that is the source of the tree, and it is the root that sustains the visible tree.

그리고 울면서 25만 원인가 하는 정성금과 함께 쌀 한 말과 초를 가져왔습니다. 돌아가신 이소저 할머니가 서울에서 여관 하실 때죠.

그런데 그때는 지금처럼 여러분한테 마음공부를 가르치지 않았을 때입니다. 당사자가 마음공부를 통해 스스로 어떻게 해 볼 수가 없으니 당장 그 울고불고하며 고통받는 거나 없애 줘야겠다고 생각을 했어요.

그 부인이 여관에서 며칠을 있다가 갔는데 나중에 진찰을 받으러 병원에 다시 갔더니 의사가 오진을 했다면서 돌려보냈답니다. 그리고 남편이 그 소리를 듣고는 말입니다, 오진이라는데 왜 그런 돈을 없앴느냐 하면서 돈을 찾으러 온 겁니다. 허허허.

As she cried, she gave an offering of a bag of rice, some candles, and 250,000 won. That was in, let's see, Mrs. Lee So Jeo still ran her inn in Seoul, so it would have been about 1970. Which was a lot of money for those days.[15]

Back then, I didn't teach people about relying upon their fundamental mind the way that I do now. She was crying and in pain, but didn't know anything about how to take her suffering and entrust it to her foundation. She was in so much pain that she couldn't even think about anything else, so I just took care of the outer problem that her karmic consciousnesses were causing. Once the pain was gone, she could hear what I had to say to her.

The lady stayed at Mrs. Lee's inn for several days, and went to see her doctor for another exam. As he looked at her results, he said there must have been a mistake before, because now she had no trace of leukemia. When her husband heard this, he was furious and accused her of wasting his

---

15. This would have been a bit over US $5,000 in 2015 dollars. Mrs. Lee So Jeo would later donate the land for the Anyang Hanmaum Seon Center.

그런데 내가 이소저 할머니더러 이런 말을 했었어요. 쌀하고 초하고 그 보따리하고 그 여자분이 가져온 그대로 놔두라고, 그 봉투도 건드리지 말라고요. 이소저 할머니는 신도들 밥이라도 해 주면 좋겠다는 걸, 곧 쓸 데가 있을 테니 그냥 놔두라고 했었습니다.

아니나 다를까 며칠 있다 그 남편이 찾으러 온 거예요. 작정하고 돈을 찾으러 왔으니 안 주고 배길 수가 없죠? 하하하. 부처님 앞에 정성들이고 간 거를 왜 되찾으러 왔느냐 한다고 해서 이해할 사람 같으면 애초에 오지도 않았겠죠. 그렇게 돈을 도로 가져간 후 그 부인은 괜찮은데 반대로 본인이 암에 걸렸단 말입니다.

그 업식이라는 거는, 본인 스스로 자기 근본자리에서 해결하지 않으면 절대 면치 못하는 겁니다. 당장 벌어진 이거를 없애면 저게 생기고, 저거를 없애면 이게 생기고 이러는 겁니다. 근본적으로 없애지 않으면 그게 그렇게 될 수밖에 없어요. 또 이게, 인연되어진 모든 것들과 연결되어 있는 거지 어디 하나에만 종속되어 있는 게 아닙니다. 결국 그 남자

money. He came up to Seoul and demanded the money, so I just gave it back.

Prior to this, I had told Mrs. Lee to just leave it there, wrapped up just as the lady had brought it. Mrs. Lee suggested using the rice to feed visitors, but I told her that someone would soon be coming for it.

As I had anticipated, he came demanding the money, ready to start throwing his fists around. So I just gave it to him, of course. It was like a child who eats an ice cream and then demands his money back because now he doesn't have any ice cream. What can you do but shake your head?

How could you come demanding offerings made to the Buddha? Of course, if he could have understood this point, he wouldn't have behaved like that in the first place. Although his wife recovered and was fine, he later ended up coming down with cancer. For when he took back her offering, he also took with him all the unseen causes of her illness.

As I've said before, it's the functioning of karmic states of consciousness that causes these kinds of things. These karmic consciousnesses…,

는 행패를 부리며 돈을 그렇게 찾아가고는 염치가 없는지 못 오더군요.

그 후에 어느 신도분이 그러길 "그 부인이 어린애 못 낳아 고생할 때도 낳도록 도와주시고, 정신이 불안정한 것도 잡아 주시고, 또 백혈병도 낫게 해 주셨는데 그 남편도 좀 도와주시죠." 하더군요.

하지만 내가 뭐, 병원의 의사입니까? 그래도 마음으로는 안됐어서, 그저 감자 물이라도 해 잡수면 좋겠다고 했습니다. 물론 그 감자 물이 낫게 하는 거는 아닙니다만 마음을 같이 내 드린 거지요. 아직까지 살아있다는 소식은 들었습니다. 우리가 살다 보면 이런 저런 일을 겪습니다. 때론 어처구니없고 섭섭한 일이 생기기도 하지요. 그렇다고 해서 상대방 못되라고 마음을 쓰시는 안 돼요. 그것도 다 업이 됩니다. 그저 모든 걸 내 주인공, 내 근본마음에 놓고 가세요.

you have to dissolve them yourself, through your foundation. Otherwise, they'll always hunt you down. Even if you take care of one aspect, they just pop up later with a different form. These karmic states are woven throughout all your relationships and history, so there's not just one cause for what you're experiencing. Anyway, the poor man was so ashamed of how he behaved that he never did come see me again, even when he was sick.

A while later a friend of the couple happened to visit me. During our conversation, she said, "You've helped them so much in the past, can't you do something now? When she had severe depression, you helped her. When she couldn't get pregnant, you helped her. And when she came down with leukemia, you helped her. Can't you do something for her husband now?"

My first thought was, "There's nothing more I can do for him." But he was in so much pain, so I told her that if he couldn't keep anything else down, then drinking potato juice everyday might help him. Does that sound like some special medicine? No. But with it, I entrusted the thought that he should recover. And the last I heard, he's

죽고 사는 걸 떠나야만이 진실한 믿음이 됩니다. 이 근본마음은 수억 겁 광년 전에도 있었고, 과거 미생물에서부터 나를 형성시키고 진화시켜, 쫓고 쫓기면서 지금의 나를 있게 한 겁니다. 이렇게 나를 끌고 온 장본인을 믿고 일체를 맡기세요.

만약 죽는게 두렵고 살아야겠다는 생각만 한다면 진화는 어떻게 합니까? 자기 부처, 자기 근본마음을 믿고, 거기에 몰락 맡기고 가십시오.

올팡갈팡하는 믿음은 믿음이 아닙니다. 모든 걸 거기서 형성시킨 것이니 고치는 것도 거기서만이 할 수 있다는 믿음을 가지십시오. 마음으로 병난 거는 마음으로 해결을 해야 하고, 육신이 병난 거는 육신으로 대처를 해 가며 병원에서 잘 고치도록 하세요. 자기 주인공을 믿고 일체를 그 자리에 맡기면 의사와도 잘 통하게 돼서 치료가 좀 수월해집니다.

still alive. In any event, no matter how badly someone else behaves, no matter what suffering they cause you, never, ever raise a thought that they should suffer or come to harm.

Only when you let go of even whether you live or die, will true faith arise. Only then will you begin to know unwavering faith in your foundation. This fundamental mind of yours existed trillions of years ago, it formed you from microbes, and even as you passed through an endless cycle of eating and being eaten, it helped you evolve to where you are now. Yet people go through life not trusting this foundation. This foundation that's been guiding them all this time.

If you give in to fears about death and desperately try to cling to life, then even after you die, even though you've entered the process of dying and being reborn, you'll still have a hard time evolving. So have faith in your inner Buddha, your foundation, and completely entrust it with everything.

Flip flopping around isn't faith. This foundation has given rise to you, so know that it can also take care of you, and go forward. For illness of the

그리고 사실 병원에서 하는 역할처럼 물질적인 것들도 중요해요. 만물이 있기에 이 마음의 파장도 전달 전달되면서 무언가로 확립이 되는 거니까요. 그런데 우리가 이 전달 과정을 보면 정말 한순간이에요.

자가발전소 같은 이 근본마음에서 한번 생각을 내면 두뇌로 해서 **사대(四大)**[12]로 그냥 전파가 되고 통신이 됩니다. 이렇게 통신이 되면 몸속의 모든 생명들이 그대로 따라 주니까 일사불란하게 주위를 다 살펴 줄 수가 있어요. 마음은 체가 없으니 자유자재로 들고 나면서 말이에요. 이렇게 되면 모든 의식들이 한마음이 되어, 내 몸과 내 부처를 동시에 적절히 모시게 되죠.

---

12. 사대(四大): 불교에서는 사람의 몸이 지·수·화·풍이라는 네 가지 물질적 요소로 성립되었다 보고 있으므로, 여기에서 사대란 곧, 인간의 신체를 일컬음.

mind, cure them through mind, for problems of the flesh, take care of your body and make wise use of doctors and hospitals. If you entrust everything – the pain, the illness, the doctor who wants to treat you – to your Juingong, then energy and understanding will flow back and forth between your foundation and the people treating you. And so, your treatment will go much smoother.

Using the material aspect to take care of things is also important. This world and ourselves are composed of every kind of matter and energy, and through this, the intentions arising from our fundamental mind spread out like a wave and manifest into the world. This transmission is so fast, there's no gap between sending and receiving.

When we raise an intention from our foundation, the energy that comes from this is so powerful, it's like there is a massive power plant within us generating it. Like energy sent out along power lines, or radio and TV waves showing up in our homes, when we raise a thought from our foundation, it goes out through our brain to all the parts of our body, communicating with them all.

In this way, all these lives that make up our body can function together as one, according to the

작년인가 재작년에 어느 고등학생이 이런 말을 했습니다. 집에 가는 길에 골목길에서 열댓 명쯤 되는 불량배 애들한테 칼로 위협을 당한 적이 있었는데, 그 상황이 무서우니까 몸이 얼어서 멍청하게 서 있기만 했답니다. 그러면서도 한편으론 내가 일러준 게 생각나서 진심을 다해 '아이고, 주인공! 아이고, 스님!' 이랬대요. 급하니까요. 그랬는데 그 애들이 자기 몸을 위아래로 다 뒤지고는 주머니에 있던 만 원만 가져가고 욕만 하더니 발길질 한 번 안 하고 갔답니다.

아무것도 모르고 그냥 선원에만 다녔는데 '야, 이런 거구나!' 하는 생각이 들었대요. 그 모든 걸 여기다가, 내 주인공 자리에 급하니까 이것저것 따지지 않고 확 맡겨 버리니, 보이지 않는 내 안의 의식들이 나를 지키고자 하는 마음으로 하나가 되는 겁니다. 그렇게 마음이 하나로 뭉쳐지니 그게 상대방 마음에 전달이 되어 악한 마음을 순간이나마 선하게 해 놓는 거예요. 그러면 해치지 않고 그냥 가게 돼요.

intention we give rise to. Further, because neither the mind nor consciousnesses of these lives have physical form, they can freely go back and forth from our body, examining the situation around us and taking care of it. If all the lives within us become one like this, then each understands that, "I am Buddha. I am all unenlightened beings. And so, I need to take care of them all."

A high school boy who comes to the Seon center had an experience like this not too long ago. He was taking a shortcut through a back street when some older boys suddenly pulled knives on him and demanded all his money. He was so surprised and shocked that he just stood there, frozen. But he thought about what he'd heard here, and silently, sincerely, called out, "Juingong! Kun Sunim!" because he was so desperate. They turned his pockets inside out, but all he had with him was 10,000 won(about US $10). Instead of beating him up, they just swore at him and left.

He told me that until then he'd just followed his parents to the Seon center, and had never practiced entrusting anything. All he'd done was listen to my talk about entrusting until that moment when

그러니 이렇게 할 수 있다는 믿음, 이 이치를 알고 모르고를 떠나 이런 믿음을 가져야 하지 않겠습니까? 그런데 경전을 달달 외우고 학술적인, 지식적인 뭔가를 머리에 잔뜩 채우고는 관습에 딱 죄여서 인이 되어 박히니 사람이 아주 약아지고 '요건 된다, 요건 안 된다'가 아주 뚜렷해지는 거예요. 자기가 아는 상식으로 이러이러하다는 게 틀이 딱 박혀서 '믿음' 이런 건 확실히 들어가지 못하는 거죠.

그래서 석가모니 부처님께서도 그러시길, 좀 무식하고 바보 같아야 자기 근본을 더 빠르게 믿게 된다고 하셨습니다. 설불리 아는 게 많으면 망설이는 게 많거든요. '이게 정말인가? 이거 거짓 아니야?' 이러는데, 거짓이고 아니고 따질 게 뭐 있습니까? 자기가 자기 믿으라는데요.

he was desperate. The urgency of the situation focused him on entrusting that confrontation to Juingong.

So the consciousnesses of the lives that make up his body all became one, and were focused on protecting him. They went and changed the vicious intentions of those young men into a kinder state, so that they just left the boy there, without hurting him. Now he understands the power of entrusting!

You need this kind of unconditional trust in this inherent Buddha essence of yours. This has to underlie everything else. Yet so many people get caught up in trying to accumulate knowledge – memorizing the sutras, studying others' theories, cleverly dissecting out different points, and so on. They end up thinking they know something, but all they've done is make everything fit the framework of their own fixed ideas. Despite how clever they appear, people like this have a hard time actually developing deep faith in their foundation.

This is why Sakyamuni Buddha said that those people without much education or cleverness are often able to have much deeper faith in their foundation, and so make more progress in their practice. Sometimes people with a lot of

타의(他意)의 어떤 형상이나 무언가를 믿으라고 해야 '이게 도대체 맞는 건가? 어떻게 되는 거지?' 하고 따지고 살피는 거지, 자기 자신을 믿으라는데 뭐 그리 따집니까? 그렇지 않습니까? 누구 몸뚱이를 믿으라는 것도, 이름을 믿으라는 것도, 허공을 믿으라는 것도 아니고, 못났든 잘났든 자기를 있게 한 자기 근본을 믿으라는데 말이에요. 내가 이 세상에 나왔으니 세상이 있는 거고, 희로애락, 이 모든 게 있는 겁니다. 자기 근본이 주체예요.

　　그래서 자기 근본, 자기 자신을 알라고 하는 겁니다. 그러니까 또 어떤 이들은 좌선을 해야만 그 깨달음을 얻는 줄 알고 그렇게들 하고 있는데, 그게 아니에요. 그냥 생활 자체, 우리가 나고 죽고 생활하는 게 그대로 불교고, 그대로 불법이고, 그대로 참선이고, 그대로 공안(公案)이고, 그대로 **여여(如如)**[13]함입니다. 그거를 아시고 생활 속에서, 내가 가

---

13. 여여(如如): 만물만생이 평등하고 차별 없이, 어디에도 머물지 않고 끊임없이 흘러 돌아가고 있는 그대로의 모습. 일체가 고정됨이 없이 돌아가는 진실의 모습을 말하며, 이러한 진리의 흐름에 부합하는 삶을 살아가는 것을 여여한 삶이라 함.

knowledge tend to get caught up in scepticism, and are suspicious of everything. But what is there to doubt when it comes to believing in what you truly are?

If I was telling you to believe in someone else, or to believe in their power, then you might want to step carefully. But I'm not. I'm telling you to believe in your own foundation, your fundamental essence, which has been leading you forward for eons. I'm not telling to rely on other's flesh nor to put your faith in lofty titles, nor to believe in some place up in the sky. Your inherent nature is what led you to be born into this world, and through which you perceive and experience everything. So trust this. Regardless of where you are in your life, of how things are going, trust your true self.

This is why I'm always saying that you have to know your foundation, what you truly are. However, sometimes people treat sitting meditation as if it was some inherent, unique truth that could awaken them to the *Buddha-dharma*,[16]

---

16. Buddha-dharma: This can refer to the fundamental reality that the teachings of Buddha point towards, or, occasionally, the teachings themselves.

고 오는 데서 이 도리를 깨달아야 하지 않을까 이런 생각을 합니다.

　우리가 '주인공(主人空)' 이럴 때 이 '공(空)' 자가 들어간 거는 뭐냐? 이 세상에 고정되어 있는 게 하나도 없기 때문에 들어가 있는 겁니다. 그래서 '세상은 공했다!' 이러는 거고요.

　고정되게 한 가지만을 보는 것도 아니고, 한 가지만을 듣는 것도 아닙니다. 그저 찰나찰나 이것도 보고 저것도 보고, 이 소리도 듣고 저 소리도 들으면서 마음도 같이 이렇게 저렇게 달라지는 겁니다. 마음이 그냥 아주 시공을 초월해서 돌아가요.

but this isn't the case. Everything you encounter, everything you go through each day, all of the living and dying, is Buddhism in its entirety. It is the Buddha-dharma, meditation, kong-ans, and *true suchness*.[17] Know this: It is through all the things and experiences of your daily life that awakening can be found.

In the word, "Juingong," the character for "gong(空)" means "*emptiness*."[18] Because everything in this world is constantly changing and flowing, with nothing that remains stationary. Nothing!

Do your eyes see only the same, one image? Do you hear only the same sound? What you see and

---

17. True suchness: Here, Daehaeng Kun Sunim is saying that everything we encounter in our daily lives is the teachings of the truth (the Buddha-dharma), a method for awakening to the truth (such as meditation and kong-ans,) and the state of being one with the truth (true suchness.)

18. Emptiness: Emptiness is not a void, but rather refers to the ceaseless flowing of all things. Everything is flowing as part of one whole, so there is nothing that can be separated out and set aside as if it existed independently of everything else. There is, therefore, no "me" that exists apart from other people or other things. There is only the interpenetrated and interdependent whole, "empty" of any independent or separate selves or objects.

The Doctor is In

그러니 이와 같이 찰나찰나 고정됨이 없이 돌아가는 도리를 그대로 참선인 줄 알고, 그대로 여여함인 줄 알고, 그대로 불교인 줄 아세요. 일상생활 그 자체가 종교인 줄 아시고 가셔야만이 그 살림살이를 이끌어 가는 나, 그 나를 있게 하는 나의 근본이 진실히 믿어지는 겁니다. 나를 형성시킨 것도 나고, 나를 죽이는 것도 나고, 나를 살리는 것도 나인데, 생사(生死)를 어디에 의지하고 누구한테 묻습니까? 그 생과 사 가운데에 마음이 (손가락을 하나 세워 보이시며), 움죽거리는 마음이 있습니다.

사람으로 진화하여 이 세상에 태어나 그저 사는 날까지 열심히 살아도 한 번 병들면 쓰러지니 그뿐입니다. 보잘것없죠. 사람 인생이라는 게 얼마나 보잘것없는지 모릅니다. 우리가 하루살이를 볼 때 어떤 생각이 듭니까? 그리고 저 산천초목이, 저 산봉우리가 우리를 볼 때 또 어떻게 볼 것 같습니까? 금강산에 있는 일만 이천 봉이 우리를 볼 때 어떻게 보겠느냐 이거죠. 하루살이 같겠죠? 몸뚱아리 하나만 보면 그래요.

hear constantly changes, doesn't it? You hear one thing, then another, and then something else. And your thoughts and feelings change accordingly. Instantly going to the past, the future, and every kind of place.

This continuous flowing of the whole, of everything, is itself meditation, true suchness, Buddhism, and is the true meaning of religion. All of this is right here, in every part of your life. When you try to live like this, then you will come to know your true nature – your true essence – and see that it's leading you forward every moment. You will begin to realize that this foundation is what causes you to exist, what lets you die, and what lets you take shape again. What else is there that you think someone else can do for you? There, in the midst of living, of becoming, and disappearing, all is done by mind. [Holding up one finger.]

No matter how hard we worked to be born as a human being, no matter how diligently we live, all it takes is one illness, and everything's over. It takes so little to bring this human life to an end. It's so tenuous. What do the mountains and great trees think about us as we pass by? Walking through the

그런데 우리 인간이 그냥은 아니에요. 어떤 사람들은 '예전에 우리 조상들은 사는 게 얼마나 힘들었을까? 지금 세상은 이렇게 편리하고 좋은데…'라고 하면서 안타까워하는데 그 조상들이 과거에 나서 죽은 거로 머물러 있는 게 아닙니다. 지금 현재에 이미 나왔기 때문에 그때 그 조상들은 못살았느니 못 먹었느니 할 것도 없어요. 우리가 아는 일만 이천 봉이나 팔만 구 암자에 많은 뜻이 담겨 있는 것처럼 우리 인간도 그렇습니다. 온갖 것을 다 겪으며 지금까지 온 거라서 거기엔 과거, 현재, 미래가 다 있어요.

옛날에 있었던 그 모든 얘기도 현실 얘기고 미래의 얘깃거리도 바로 오늘 얘깃거리입니다. 이렇게 삼세(三世)가 같이 돌아가는 현생에서 우리가 지금 살고 있는 거예요.

forests and twelve thousand peaks of the Diamond Mountains, we must seem to them like mayflies. If all you know is this material flesh, then this certainly seems to be the case.

Someone I was talking with gave a sigh and said it was such a shame that her grandparents and great-grandparents never got to experience life in the country that Korea has become. These days, everything is so developed and prosperous, but they all lived and died during such hard times. However, our ancestors aren't frozen in the past. They're already here, now, living with us in this same world. Just as the Diamond Mountains reverberate with the energy and stories of their thousand hermitages, we have right here within us, everything that we have experienced and undergone. Even though our lives seem fragile and short, we carry everything we've done with us. All of the past, present, and even the future are right here, right now.

Everything that happened in the past is also happening right now, and everything that will happen in the future is also being created right now. We are living here in this present life together with all the past, present, and future.

그러니까 여러분이 이 공부를 진짜 하려면, 생활 속에서 근면하고 착실하고 진실하게, 내가 지금 금방 죽는다 하더라도 눈 하나 깜짝 안 하는 그런 믿음을 가지고 해야 합니다. '네가 형성시킨 거니까 네가 없애려면 없애고 좀 더 살게 하려면 더 살게 하고 네 마음대로 해!' 이런다고 잘못되는 거 없습니다.

이번 생에 이 공부를 만났는데 어차피 죽는 거 그냥 살다 죽지 말고, 이번엔 한번 나를 있게 한 내 근본마음을 믿어 보면 어떻겠습니까?

그래서 이 몸뚱이 속에 사는 모든 중생들이 전부 한마음이 돼서 부처와 둘이 아니게끔 하나로 돌아간다면 얼마나 건강하고 좋을까요? 다음 생엔 크게 진화가 되어 더 깊은 지혜를 가지고 나올 겁니다.

If you really want to become spiritually free, if you want to know how to grow and live as a true human being, then start with faith in your inherent essence. Right here, now, in your day-to-day life, diligently and honestly work at trusting this essence with whatever is going on. So that even if you were about to die, you wouldn't blink an eye. "Okay, true nature, you formed me, so if this existence is finished, then let's be done with it. If I need to continue this longer, then let's do that. You figure it out!" Even though you let go of everything like this, you won't go wrong.

At any rate, either way we are all going to die, so before that time comes, why not try to experiment with having this kind of trust in our essence? See what happens when you start living like this.

By trusting your inherent Buddha-nature with all that you're going through, the lives within your body will all begin function together as one, following the lead of your Buddha-nature. How could they not become healthy and joyous? If you can evolve like this during this life, how could you not come out at a higher level in your next life? How could you not be born with deeper wisdom and insight?

사실 따지고 보면 이 도리를 완전히 깨닫든 아니든, 공부한다는 것 자체가 엄청난 겁니다. 그렇지 않으면 아예 느껴 보지도 못하고 맛도 모를 테니까요. 역대 조사들도 그걸 모르는 중생들이 안타까워 아마 속으로는 팔짝팔짝했을 거예요. 그렇지만 어쩝니까, 본인이 해야만 알 수 있는 걸.

그러니까 안타까워도 할 수 없이 턱 놔 버리고 겉으론 그냥 편안하게 지냈겠죠, 허허허. '깡통은 깡통끼리 왈가닥왈가닥하고 살 거고, 금은 금대로 빛을 내며 살 거고, 아이고, 그대로 사는 거지 어쩌겠나!' 하고 말입니다. 우리가 사는 이 세계는 중세계(中世界)인데 자기가 어떻게 하는가에 따라 체로 쳐져서 상세계로 올라가기도 하고 하세계로 떨어지기도 합니다.

To be perfectly frank, it is an incredible thing to learn to rely upon this fundamental essence and apply its energy to the world around us. For, without doing this, you may never taste or experience this treasure that each of us has. I suspect that awakened beings have always felt frustrated as they observed the speech and actions of people who were ignorant of this treasure. Yet what could they do? No one else can do this for you. You have to want it and work for it yourself.

This is why some Seon masters just ignored the world, and lived free and easy. [Laughs.] They must have thought to themselves, "Empty tin cans bang together and make all kinds of noise. And gold gathers together with gold and shines even brighter. They will live as they will. Ho, what can someone else do about it?!" This *middle world*[19] we are now living in is like a sieve, sifting people

---

19. Middle world: In Buddhism, the realm of human beings is sometimes described as the "middle realm" or the "middle world," because it said to be one of six realms. It exists below the realms of more advanced beings, called devas and asuras, but above the realms of animals, hungry ghosts, and the various hell states.

그리고 지난번에도 얘기했지만, 지옥이라는 곳이 따로 없어요. 한 예로 독사같이 살았으면 독사의 몸을 지니고 나오는 겁니다. 그러기 때문에 이 도리가 무서운 거죠. 보이지 않는 자동적인 인과가 그렇게 무섭단 말입니다.

그런데 인간으로 살던 사람이 퇴보하여 독사로 나오게 되면 몸은 독사라도 사람으로 살던 의식이 남아 있기 때문에 사는 게 더 지옥 같은 겁니다. 그러면 더 악에 받쳐 살겠죠.

옛날에 무당들이 굿하는 걸 보니까, 칼을 휘두르고 죽을 끼얹으면서 "썩 물러가거라. 물러가지 않으면 밥내, 국내도 맡지 못하게 할 것이다." 이러더라고요. 그 말은 뭐냐 하면, 그렇게 사람한테 들러붙어서 귀찮게 굴고 못되게 굴고 그러면 지옥으로 떨어져서 지금보다도 더 못한, 땅속의 벌레가 된다는 소립니다. 자기가 산 대로 그대로 짐승이나 벌레의 모습으로 바뀌져 나온단 말입니다.

into higher or lower realms, according to how they live.

As I mentioned in the last talk, there isn't some separate place called Hell. Let me try to explain this for a bit. If you live this life like a poisonous snake, then after death that's the kind of body you will be drawn towards. This invisible, automatic process of cause and effect, and *karmic affinity*,[20] is truly fearsome.

Imagine someone who is reborn as a snake. They will have all the habits, and some of the consciousness of a human being. Yet they'll be trapped in a snake's body, with all its limitations. That right there is hell.

A long time ago, I happened to see a shaman performing an exorcism. She was dancing with a sword, waving it around and scattering bits of porridge around the yard. All the while, she was shouting, "Go away! If you don't leave now, you'll never again smell steamed rice or soup!"

---

20. Karmic affinity(因緣): The connection or attraction between people or things, due to previous karmic relationships.

지옥이 따로 있고 천당이 따로 있는 게 아니라 우리가 사는 이 세상이 지옥이고 천당입니다. 그 굿 하는 사람은 이 전체의 의미를 모르고 나오는 대로 말을 하는 거겠지만요.

보세요. 우리 이 사람이라는 게 얼마나 대단한지! 이 안에 다 있어요. **오신통(五神通)**[14]이 다 들어가 있어요. 사진기, 탐지기, 통신기, 망원경 이런 역할을 하는 게 다 있는 거죠. 천안통(天眼通), 타심통(他心通), 신족통(神足通), 천이통(天耳通), 숙명통(宿命通) 이런 게 여기 이렇게 한데 부착이 돼서 돌아가니까 이거는 뭐, 사대 팔방으로 이 허공에 전부

---

14. 오신통(五神通): 불교의 육신통(六神通) 중에서 누진통(漏盡通)을 뺀 다섯 가지의 신통(능력), 즉 천안통(天眼通), 천이통(天耳通), 타심통(他心通), 숙명통(宿命通), 신족통(神足通)을 일컬음. 천안통(天眼通)은 보는 사이 없이 볼 수 있는 능력, 천이통(天耳通)은 듣는 사이 없이 들을 수 있는 능력, 타심통(他心通)은 다른 이의 마음을 아는 사이 없이 알 수 있는 능력, 숙명통(宿命通)은 과거 어디로부터 왔는지를 아는 사이 없이 아는 능력, 신족통(神足通)은 한 찰나에 가고 옴이 없이 가고 올 수 있는 능력을 말함.

This meant that if that ghost didn't stop bothering the person it was inhabiting, then it's harmful behavior would cause it to be reborn at some low level like that of a burrowing insect, where it would be beyond contact with human beings.

Although the shaman herself didn't know the implications of what she was saying, in any event, it's true that someone who lives like an animal or insect will next take the body of an animal or insect. Both heaven and hell are right here, where we are living now.

Look at yourself for a moment. A human being is so impressive! Everything is there, including even what are called the *five subtle powers*.[21] These have all the capabilities of cameras, mobile phones, radars, and telescopes. They make it possible to see anything, to hear anything, to know others' minds, to know the past and future, and to go anywhere without moving your body. These abilities all arise from your fundamental mind,

---

21. Five subtle powers (五神通)**:** The power to know past and future lives, the power to know others' thoughts and emotions, the power to see anything, the power to hear anything, and the power to go anywhere.

The Doctor is In

연결이 돼 그냥 조달이 되는 거죠. 그러니까 하나도 깔축없이 입력되었다 나왔다 하는 겁니다. 자기가 남한테 욕을 했으면 그것이 입력이 되었다가 자기가 욕을 먹게끔 바뀌어져서 나온단 말입니다.

그러니 될 수 있으면 모든 거를 주인한테 맡기세요. 주인이 하는 거지 육신이 자기 맘대로 하는 게 아니에요. TV에서 나오는 것들은 TV란 상자가 만들어서 보여주는 게 아닌 거처럼요. 게다가 그 많은 것을 보여주는 TV가 선 하나만 끊어져도 안 나오죠? 이 육신, 이 오장육부가 바로 이와 같습니다. 또 TV에 나오는 방송들을 이것저것 다 보는 게 아니라 우리가 보고 싶은 거 보고 보기 싫은 거는 안 보고, 그렇게 보는 사람 맘대로 조절하잖아요? TV가 마음대로 하는 게 아닙니다. 그러니 뭘 믿어야 되겠어요?

내 육신은 이 오장육부가 들어 있는 집일 뿐입니다. 이번 생(生) 동안 보호하고 관리하는 곳이죠. 그리고 이 모든 건 내 의식에 의해 돌아가고 그 의식들은 근본마음에 의지합니다. 이 한마음을 중시하고 들어가거든요.

automatically communicating and bringing things together. They catch everything, so if you yell at someone or give them a hard time, that's input, and in time will cause you to create situations where you end up being yelled at.

So, as best you can, entrust everything to your essence, Juingong. It's what is doing everything; do you think your flesh is just moving around on its own? What you see on the TV isn't being made by that square box. It's a fragile thing that becomes useless if just one bit of wiring or cable is cut. Further, you're the one who makes the decisions about what that TV displays. You're the one who decides what will be seen or not seen; the TV doesn't just do that on its own. It's not the shell you should trust, but rather the essence that moves it.

All the parts of our body, all of our organs, all of our flesh, all the lives and consciousnesses that make up this body all follow this one mind. They all respond to one mind. So, if we don't truly know what's going on, if we're being swept up by circumstances, then shouldn't we be placing our trust in this foundation that has guided us this far?

표현을 잘했는지 못했는지 모르겠습니다마는 아까도 얘기했듯이 우리는 지구가 어디로 돌아다니는지 감도 잡을 수 없습니다. 지구가 태양계에서 이리 돈다고 하니 뭔가 아는 거 같지만, 어떻게 생겼는지조차 모르는 이 우주 전체가 움직이고 있으니 그 안에 있는 지구가 어디로 돌아다니는지는 알 수가 없습니다. 아십니까? 모르시죠? 모르니까 아는 데다 맡기라는 겁니다. 그게 바로 자기 근본마음이에요.

신도: 그런데 모른다는 걸 아는 게 아는 거 아닙니까?

큰스님: 하하하. 그건 자기가 모른다는 걸 아는 거겠죠. 우리 이 지구처럼 육신의 세포 하나하나의 의식들은 인간이 어디로 그렇게 돌아다니는지 모릅니다. 그러니까 근본마음을 통해 너와 내가 한 몸이라는 걸 알려 줘서, 세포의 의식들이 '아, 이렇게 다니는 것도 나구나!' 하고 믿게 하는 겁니다. 믿음이 확고하면 자기 손가락을 자기가 꺾는 일은 하지 않

Right now, our home, this earth, the solar system, and the galaxy, are all hurtling through space. Does anyone here know where we're headed? Can that ever that be known by anyone?

A member of the audience: Ah, but isn't knowing what we don't know also knowing? [Kun Sunim and the audience laugh.]

Kun Sunim: No, it pretty much just means that you don't know. [Laughs.] It's like the cells that make up this body of ours. They have no idea where the body is going or what it's doing. So, if you let them know that they and all the other cells are actually one whole body – if through your foundation, you make these consciousnesses one with you – then one part won't end up hurting another part. They'll understand that, "All of this is me!"

So, have unconditional faith in your own foundation! Whether an illness improves, or doesn't, whether things start going the way you want, or don't, trust that in all of this, your foundation is leading you forward. It guided you

죠. 다시 말해, 자기가 자기를 죽이는 일은 할 수 없는 거예요.

그러니까 내 근본마음에 대한 믿음을 가지려면 진실하고 확실하게 믿으세요. 병이 낫고 안 낫고를 떠나서, 또 되고 안 되고를 떠나서 믿어야 합니다. 수억 겁을 통해 쫓고 쫓기면서 진화를 시켜 지금 사람이 되었는데, 사람으로 태어났다고 끝이 아닙니다. 쫓고 쫓기면서 지금껏 진화한 것처럼, 또 쫓고 쫓겨야 마음이 발전이 되고 진화가 됩니다.

그래서 어떤 어려움도 공부로 알라 그러는 겁니다. 왕창 하늘이 무너진다 하더라도, 그래서 좀 허둥대는 게 있더라도 내 근본자리만큼은 믿는 게 확실해서, '허, 또 무너지게 했군!' 하고 웃으며 쳐다볼 수 있는 넉넉한 마음이 있다면 대처가 다 되게 돼 있습니다. 대충 믿는 거는 자기를 버리는 거나 한가지입니다.

자기 자성신(自性神)을 진짜로 믿어야지, 어째서 자기를 끌고 다니는 자기 자성신을 그렇게 믿지 못합니까? 이 세상에 진짜로 믿을 게 뭐 있습니까? 대신 죽어 주는 사람이 있습니까? 대신 아파 주는

through billions of years, helping you evolve into a human being while you've hunted and been hunted, pushing you to grow and change. And now, although you've been born as a human, you still haven't reached the end. Now you have to use the things banging into you to evolve your mind.

So, no matter what kind of hardship you encounter, take it as something to practice with. Even if the world were to end right now, even though you're scared and panicky, have firm trust in your foundation. If you can watch it happen and laughingly say, "What, again?" if your faith is this deep and calm, then you'll be able to manage whatever happens and guide it in a better direction. You absolutely must have faith in this essence that's been guiding you. To not have trust in it is like abandoning yourself.

You have to believe in this divine essence that exists within you. Could you really not trust this? It's what is animating you right now. What else, where else would you rely upon? Is there anyone else who can take your place when you fall ill? Is there anything else who can stand in for you when death comes? No. No matter how much your

사람이 있습니까? 자식들이 아무리 효자, 효부다 하더라도 부부지간이 아무리 정이 좋다 하더라도, 대신 똥 눠 주고, 대신 아파 주고, 대신 죽어 주고, 대신 잠자 주고 그러지는 못합니다.

수억 겁을 지나면서 인간으로 진화시킨 나의 근본마음, 자성신을 믿고 의지하면서 가세요. 믿음을 갖고 거기에 일체를 맡기면서 가야 내 마음이 진화가 되고, 또 내 가정이라도 밝게 밝힐 수 있는 지혜가 생기며 능력이 생깁니다. 그것이 바로 부처님께서 가르쳐 주신 법입니다.

질문 있으면 질문하십시오.

질문자 1(남): 제가 평소에 의문 나던 점을 몇 가지로 요약해서 말씀드리겠습니다. 현대 과학의 발달로 인간의 유전인자에 대한 비밀이 조금씩 벗겨지고 있습니다. 보도에 따르면 프랑스 과학자들이 지금까지 베일에 싸여 있던 한 유전인자의 구조를 밝혀냈다고 합니다. 그런데 이 발견이 왜 특별하냐 하면 유전인자의 구조가 밝혀짐에 따라 몇 가지 유전병의 치료 방법을 알아낼 수 있게 된 것입니다.

children love you, no matter how much your wife or husband cares for you, no one can even stand in for you when you need to use the toilet. No one can take your place when you need sleep, or are sick, or are dying.

Rely upon and trust your inherent essence. Go forward trusting this essence that has lead you across a billion eons, and worked to evolve you. If you have steadfast faith in this and entrust it with everything you experience, then your mind will rapidly evolve and the wisdom and ability you develop will cause your family to live together joyfully. Doing all this is the essence of all the Buddha's teachings.

Now, are there any questions today?

Questioner 1 (Male): I'd like to ask you about the role of science and its relationship with cause and effect. This is something I've wondered about for a while now. Science has been revealing the secrets of DNA bit by bit, and recent journal articles reported that a French team has uncovered an aspect of genes that they believe will be the key to treating genetic diseases. They report that

과학자들의 말로는 앞으로 20여 년 후면 수천 가지의 유전병과 불치병 중에 상당한 부분의 치료법이 개발될 거라고 합니다.

그렇다면 여기서 한 가지 의문이 떠오릅니다. 제가 알기로는 유전병 또는 불치병은 억겁을 거쳐 오는 동안의 인과가 뭉친 결과라고 알고 있습니다만, 마음법이 아니라 물리적인 방법, 즉 과학적인 치료법으로도 인과를 녹이는 이치가 있는 것인지 궁금합니다.

가령 이와 같은 과학적인 방법으로 유전자의 비밀이 밝혀진다면 과학이 보이지 않는 세계로 넘나드는 일이 되며, 나아가서는 인과의 법칙도 새로운 해석을 해야 하는 게 아닌지 궁금합니다.

큰스님: 아무리 과학자들이 치료법을 발견했다 하더라도 그건 당장 보여진 어떤 병에 대한 치료 물질일 뿐입니다. 어디서, 왜, 어떠한 연관성으로 그러한 유전병이 왔느냐 하는 걸 모르기 때문에, 그 유전병을 고쳤다 하더라도 병을 일으킨 원인이 없어지

within the next twenty years or so, this will make it possible for us to treat thousands of previously incurable genetic diseases.

If this is true, then I have a question. As I understand it, genetic diseases and incurable diseases are the accumulated results of what we've done over the eons. Is there really a way for science to overcome these results of cause and effect?

It seems that if science can fix this through an understanding of genetics, then it can subsume this unseen realm of mind and the results of that energy. If so, it seems like a new understanding of cause and effect is necessary.

Kun Sunim: No matter how wondrous a treatment scientists have discovered, it is still only dealing with the physical, material issues that are presenting at that moment in time. But those doctors don't truly know why or how that genetic disease arose, nor all of the things connected with it. So even if they think they cured it, the underlying issues still haven't been eliminated. In the case of problems caused by karma, they will

는 게 아니에요. 인과로 온 거는 어떤 형태로든 그 이름을 떠나서 다른 거로 옮겨 나타납니다.

그렇기 때문에 근본마음으로 들어가 그 원인을 녹이는 수밖에 없어요. 입력이 된 데다가 입력을 다시 해야 그 전에 입력된 것이 없어지지, 그렇지 않으면 그것은 절대로 없어지지 않습니다.

그래서 근본마음에 모든 걸 다 놓으라는 거예요. 그렇게 맡겨 놓고 가다 보면 이 근본마음, 참나를 알게 되고, 그러면 모두가 오고 감이 없이 오고 가며 하나로 같이 돌아간다는 걸 알게 될 겁니다. 태양이 돼서 태양을 보고, 태양계를 본다는 것과 비슷해요. 그 속에서 속속들이 알게 되는 거죠. 그 병의 치료법을 발견했다고 해서 다 밝혀낸 게 아닙니다.

예를 들어서, 식물에 벌레가 자꾸 끼니까 독한 약을 줘서 다 죽였단 말이에요. 처음에는 죽었어요. 그런데 그 벌레가 '아, 저런 수를 내서 날 이렇게 하는구나.' 하고 안단 말입니다. 그렇게 살 궁리를 하니 나중에는 딴 거로 대치가 되니까 그 전 약으로는 해결이 안 되죠.

reappear as a new kind of suffering, with different names.

Thus, you have to return to your fundamental mind and dissolve those causes there. If you want to truly erase data, you record something new over the top of it, right? Otherwise, there's still something left behind. And that won't just disappear on its own.

This is why I always say, "You have to let go of everything to your fundamental mind." Then, once you know your fundamental mind, your true self, you'll see how it functions as one with everything. If you become one with the sun, you will see things from the perspective of the sun, and will truly understand the mechanics and functioning of the rest of the solar system.

Yet if you don't know where a disease came from, if you don't truly know the conditions that caused it to arise, then even though you come up with a theory or treatment for it, you won't be able to truly cure it.

Let me give you an example. When farmers have problems with insects destroying their crops, they spray them with pesticides. At first this kills

인과성이나 유전성, 세균성, 영계성 등으로 오는 여러 가지들 때문에 사람들의 정신과 육체가 약하게 되고 혼란스럽게 되는 경우가 많습니다. 이렇게 직접적으로 간접적으로 주위 모든 것에 영향을 주는데 그 연결되어 벌어지는 게 한두 가지가 아니고 다 연관성이 있는 겁니다. 병들도 새로운 것들이 생겨나서 이름이 붙여지고 그럽니다. 그런데 이런 것들이 본래부터, 전자에부터 있었던 게 아니거든요. 백혈병이다 골수암이다 이런 것도 원래부터 있었던 게 아니에요. 그래서 하는 말입니다. 그것을 박차고 나갈 수 있는 힘이 있다면, 내 근본을 믿고 그 자리에 완전히 되놓을 수 있다면 그건 없는 게 되는 거예요.

내 마음으로 내 육체 안에 들어 있는 그 모든 의식들을 다 흡수해서 작용할 수만 있다면 암이다 뭐다 하는 건 이름일 뿐이게 되고, 실질적으로 실무자들이 똥 마려우면 똥 누는 것과 같은, 그냥 자연스러운 작용으로 해결된다는 겁니다.

off the bugs. However, those bugs know what hurt them, so they try to think about how they can survive. With that intention, they begin to change and are reborn with an altered form, and so those pesticides become less and less effective.

Karma, genetics, microbes, ghosts and such can cause people to become confused, or to lose their faith. To say nothing of their influence on all kinds of other things in a person's life. Similarly, there are all kinds of new names of diseases, names that fill people with fear. Names that didn't exist in the past, such as leukemia, bone marrow cancer, and so on. If you can gather your strength and kick out the fear and confusion these inspire, entrusting the situation to your foundation, it will likely disappear.

All those names are just letters of the alphabet. If, through your fundamental mind, you can encompass all the lives in your body, such that they all work together as one, then "cancer," or whatever, just becomes empty letters. Just like you go to the toilet when you feel pressure in your bowels, the cells and lives in your body will respond to what's going on, and work all together, naturally, to take care of it.

질문자 2(남): 첨단 과학이 발달한 요즘에도 현대 의학으로는 치료가 되지 않는 병들이 우리 주위에 많습니다. 그런데 이런 불치병으로 고생하던 환자가 큰스님의 가르침을 받고 공부하다 보면 불가사의하게도 완쾌되는 경우가 주위에 많이 있습니다.

물론 이는 큰스님의 법력의 힘이라고 막연히는 믿지만, 그 심오한 치료법의 비결이 궁금합니다. 아울러 이 자리에 함께한 모든 도반들이 병고에 시달림 없이 늘 건강한 상태로 함께 공부할 수 있도록 큰스님의 법력으로 포용해 주십시오.

큰스님: 허허허, 내가 항시 여러분한테 얘기하죠? 그건 나도 아니고 여러분도 아니에요. 단 하나 있다면 마음이 오고 가면서 둘이 아니게 한데 합쳐지니까 불이 들어올 뿐입니다. 그러니까 내가 낫게 해 줬다, 네가 낫게 했다 이런 게 없어요. 그 없는 가운데 '불'이 밝혀진 거예요.

Questioner 2 (Male): Although this is supposedly the era of cutting edge science, there are still so many diseases doctors can't cure, nor even alleviate. Yet, to my surprise, I've seen diseases like these disappear almost magically when people began to apply your teachings.

Of course, I suspect the spiritual power arising from your own practice played a role, but I was wondering if you could tell us the secret by which these people were cured. And, um, since I'm here, could you please embrace all of us with your spiritual power so that we may always practice without being distracted by disease?

Kun Sunim: [Laughs.] As I've always told you, it's neither me nor you who cures the disease. If it can be said to be anything, it is this nondual mind, flowing back and forth. It's like the lights coming on when electricity flows through the whole that the light bulbs, wiring and switch. There's no "me" that cures, nor is there a "you" who recovers. In the midst of this combined whole, there is only light that becomes brighter.

여러분도 그렇게 하셔야만이 아주 돈독한 자기 자아부처의 완성을 이룰 수 있을 겁니다.

질문자 2: 아울러서 병 문제이기 때문에 감히 제 사적인 이야기를 간단히 올리겠습니다. 6, 7년 전부터 다리의 근육이 풀려 힘이 없어지는 그런 병을 앓고 있습니다. 게다가 양쪽 발 엄지발가락에 발톱이 나오기만 하면 바스러졌습니다. 이유를 몰랐죠. 그런데 금년에 와서 작은 변화가 있었습니다. 언제부턴가 발톱이 말짱하게 원형을 만들어 가고 있었습니다. 지금도 조금은 불편합니다만 양쪽 발톱이 전부 나와서 제 모양을 하고 있습니다. 좋은 징조인지요?

큰스님: 하하하. 아, 그거야 물론이죠. 물론이고말고요. 이 공부라는 게 얼마나 좋은 건지, 여북하면 부처님께서 "세세생생에 내 몸뚱이, 이 고깃덩어리가 없어도 너희가 있다면 내가 있는 것이니 열심히 그 무아(無我)의 경지에 이르러라." 하고 말씀하셨겠습니까?

This is how you have to practice. Only then can you complete yourself. Only then can you realize the potential of this incredibly close, friendly Buddha you all have within you.

Questioner 2: Since we're on the topic of disease, about six or seven years ago my legs started getting weaker and weaker. Further, my big toenails would break off as they grew out. I have no idea why this happened. However, around the beginning of this year, I started to see some changes. Now instead of breaking off, my toenails are growing out properly. I still have some discomfort, but, they're much better than before. I guess this means the rest of my body is improving as well?

Kun Sunim: [Laughs.] Of course, of course! This practice of relying upon and discovering our fundamental essence is so amazing! This practice is such a wondrous thing, with so much potential. Thus the Buddha said, "Even when this flesh of mine no longer exists, if you exist, I will be there with you, regardless of the era. So be diligent and awaken to the realm of no-self."

이 몸속에 있는 모든 것에는 마음이 있는데 이게 제각각입니다. 과거에 어떻게 살았느냐에 따라 입력된 것들이 업식이 되어 상황에 따라 이거 내보내고 저거 내보내고 그러거든요. 그러니 때에 따라 도둑질을 하려고 하기도 하고, 사기를 치려고 하기도 하고, 또 좋은 일을 하려고 하기도 해요.

그런데 이렇게 마음대로 마음을 낼 수 있는 이놈이 무엇이 나쁘고 좋고, 잘되고 못되는 건지를 안단 말입니다. 그러니까 알고 있는 이놈이 선장이 돼서 다스려라 이겁니다.

잘 다스려서 과거에 입력되었던 것이 나오는 그 자리에 되돌려 놔라 이겁니다. 그 자리에 되놓으면 모든 것이 서로 통신이 돼 선장의 뜻에 따라 주게 돼 있어요. 다 따라 주게 돼 있으니까 모자라는 건 채워 가며 이렇게 되놓는 걸 자꾸 하다 보면 몸이 좋아질 수밖에 없습니다.

All the lives within your body have their own respective consciousness, and each was recorded, each was created, according to how we were living at that moment in time. And then they come back out according to circumstances and fill our awareness. So, for no reason at all, you may suddenly feel the desire to steal something, or to deceive someone, or to do something nice, and so forth.

Yet beneath all of these is something that is able to know what is truly good, what is bad, and what will make things go better or worse. We have to make this essence the captain of our ship, so that it's able to manage and take care of everything we encounter.

We can make this happen by returning everything back place it came from. If you return it all inwardly, those karmic states of consciousness become one with this captain, your fundamental mind. They become one, and so the captain can communicate with them. Because the captain is communicating with them, they follow the captain. As these consciousnesses of the lives within you begin to follow the captain, the parts of

예전에는 소아마비나 뇌염에 걸리는 사람들이 많았었어요. 그때 오던 아이 하나가 그런 병에 걸려 고생을 했는데 아이 엄마한테 이 도리를 일러 주었더니 둘 다 공부를 아주 열심히 잘했습니다. 그래서 가늘었던 다리가 튼튼해지고 건강하게 성장해 지금은 큰 회사에 취직하여 잘 살고 있습니다.

이런 경우가 한둘이 아닙니다. 이 도리를 알아 스스로 공부를 잘하고 가면 힘들지 않게 살 수 있으니 나도 기쁘고 본인들도 기쁘고 세세생생에 좋은 거 아닙니까? 이런 예들을 본보기 삼아 자기 마음을 발전시켜 나가세요.

자기 안에 자기를 이끌고 가는 선장이 있다는 것도 알았고, 선장이 그렇게 생각을 하면 자생중생들이 다 따라 준다는 것도 알았고, 또 같이 움직여 준다는 것도 알았으니 계속 가다 보면 점차적으로 모든 자생중생들한테 항복을 받게 됩니다.

your body that were weak become stronger, and parts that were too strong begin to settle down. So, as you keep returning everything, your body will naturally become healthier.

Years ago in Korea, there were so many people who suffered from polio or encephalitis. At that time the son of a member here came down with one of those. So I taught him and his mother this, and both practiced diligently. His legs were painfully thin, but gradually they filled out and became quite strong. He grew into a healthy adult, and got a job at a big company, and now lives quite well.

There are many people here who have had similar experiences. When others can grow and live well like this, it makes me so happy! They too, are happy, and the ability they develop to trust in their foundation will bring them blessings for life after life. Take other's successful examples and use those to improve your own practice and deepen yourself.

You've learned that there is this captain, that it exists within you, and that all the lives and consciousnesses that make up your body will follow the thoughts of this captain, so, if you

항복을 받는다는 게 다시 말해 하나가 된다는 뜻이에요. 이렇게 하나가 되면 항복받은 것도 없고 안 받은 것도 없게 되니 나중에는 그대로 여여하게 됩니다.

그런데 이게 빨리 안 된다고 조급하게 생각하지는 마십시오. 저 사람은 '저렇게 빨리 되는 데 난 왜 이렇게 빨리 안 되나?' 이런 생각은 마시고 내가 이 공부를 꼭 해야겠다는 결심으로 계속하다 보면 빛도 보일 수가 있고, 어떤 땐 들릴 수도 있고, 어떤 때는 가고 옴이 없이 가고 올 수도 있는 그런 경지에 이르기도 합니다.

하지만 그런 거에 착을 두지 말고, '아, 나를 이끌어 주고 공부 가르치기 위해서 이렇게 보이고 들리고 하는구나.' 하고 감사하게 생각하고 또 되돌려 놔야 합니다. 거기에 끄달리지 말아야 합니다. 오신통(五神通)도 벗어나야 하니까 말이에요.

keep working on entrusting everything you feel and are going through to this captain, those lives responsible for that will surrender and follow the captain.

To explain "surrender" another way, all of those lives will become one with the captain, your fundamental Buddha essence. If you keep surrendering those consciousnesses to your captain, then later because they all become one, you'll find that there was nothing that surrendered, and nothing that accepted the surrender. There is only suchness, where all things are complete just as they are.

That said, be patient even when it seems like your progress is slow. Don't get caught up in comparing yourself to others or wondering why you can't do the same things they can. Just keep working at your own practice with a firm resolution. As you do this, you'll experience things you've only heard about, such as seeing auras, hearing things from faraway, or being able to leave your body and go somewhere else.

When you experience these things, be sure to let go and entrust them to your foundation. Be

오신통, 이게 (법상 위의 물컵을 가리키시며) 오신통이라면은 이 바깥으로 벗어나야 마음대로 굴리고 마음대로 먹을 수가 있지, 이 안에 들어가서는 그렇게 할 수 없지요. 그렇지 않은가요?

이 오신통이라는 것이 내 모든 법 테두리 안에서 헤어나지 못하는 이 차안(此岸) 속입니다. 차안의 속! 이 차안을 벗어나 피안(彼岸)의 세계로 나아가야 이 통을 굴린단 말입니다. 이 삼천대천세계를 굴릴 수 있다 이 소립니다.

그러니 따지고 보면 이게 엄청난 공부입니다. 웬만한 사람들은 엄두가 나지 않아 시작도 해 볼 수 없는 공부입니다. 머리 깎고 승려가 돼야만이 할 수 있다고 하는 이 공부를 여러분이 지금 하고 있는 겁니다. 예전에 사십구 년 동안 석가모니 부처님께서 설해 주실 때의 그 뜻을 안다면, 유마힐 거사나 부처님이나 다 같은 한 도량 안에서 모두 구속되지 않고 자유인으로서 중생들을 이끌어 갔던 그 뜻을 안다면 여러분들도 이 공부를 충분히 하실 수 있습니다.

grateful, and know that those experiences are there to teach you, but, nonetheless, return them inwardly. You must not cling to those or try to cultivate them. You have to be free from even the five subtle powers.

Think of this cup [holding up a cup of water] as the five subtle powers. If you want to lift it up, if you want to drink from it, you have to be outside of it, don't you? If you were in the cup, you couldn't do anything with it.

To put it another way, the five subtle powers are not the far shore of enlightenment. They exist only on this side of the river, within the realms of *ignorance*.[22] Achieving them is not enlightenment. Once we cross over to the far shore, then we can use these and anything else we need as we respond to and take care of the entire universe.

When I think of everything that's possible through this practice of working through our

---

22. Ignorance (無明)**:** In Buddhism, "ignorance" literally means darkness. It is the unenlightened mind that does not see the truth. It is being unaware of the inherent oneness of all things, and it is the fundamental cause of birth, aging, sickness, and death.

여러분한테 말없이 그 뜻을 전달하기 위해 유마힐거사도 그렇게 이 세상에 났던 겁니다. "중생들이 다 나아야 내가 낫지."라는 유마힐거사의 말씀을 '밖에 있는 중생들을 다 낫게 해야 내가 낫는다.'는 소리로 착각을 하고 있는 분들이 계시는데 그건 '내 속의 중생들이, 내 속의 생명들이 건장해야 내가, 내 몸뚱이가 건장하지 않겠는가.' 하는 뜻입니다.

벽을 치면 **봇장**[15]이 울려야지 친 것만 보고 있으면 어디 진전이 있겠습니까?

---

15. 봇장: 들보 혹은 대들보의 다른 말. 집을 지을 때에 칸과 칸 사이의 두 기둥을 가로지르는 나무. 도리와는 'ㄴ' 자로, 마룻대와는 '+' 자 모양을 이루는 나무.

fundamental essence, it's just so incredible and powerful! Most ordinary people can't even conceive of its potential, let alone try to practice it like you all are. In the past, only those who cut off all attachments and became monks or nuns could learn this. However, if you understand what the Buddha spent forty-nine years teaching, if you understand the meaning of why the Buddha and Vimalakirti worked together to guide unenlightened beings to freedom, then you're fully capable of doing this practice.

Vimalakirti, too, appeared in this world in order to show ordinary people that they too can practice and awaken.

When he said "I will become well only after all those beings suffering illness have been cured," people often misunderstood this to mean all beings throughout the universe. However, what he meant is that you have to save the unenlightened beings within you. When these lives within you become strong and robust, then won't your whole body become healthy?

That said, there's Korean saying that if you hit the wall, the rafters should shake. There are two

질문자 2: 열심히 정진하겠습니다.

큰스님: 감사합니다. 제가 외려 감사합니다. 될 수 있으면 그저 튼튼한 다리가 되서서 이 세상을 활보하신다면 더더욱 좋겠죠.

질문자 3(남): 저는 심성과학원 의학부에 소속돼 있는 정신과 의사입니다. 질문을 허락해 주셔서 감사합니다. 지금 제가 이 자리에서 질문드리고 싶은 것은 환자들 치료에 관한 부분입니다.

정신과 질환 영역에서 제일 환자가 많은 게 정신분열증입니다. 환자 수도 많고 치료도 잘 안 되는 병으로 알고 있습니다. 소위 미친 사람으로 분류가 되는 그런 사람들인데요, 우리나라 인구의 한 1%에 해당이 됩니다. 환청도 있고 망상도 보이는데 이게 갑자기 시작될 수도 있고, 차차 시작이 될 수도 있습니다. 하지만 결국 황폐해져 나중에는 사람 구실을 잘 못하게 되는 그런 과정을 밟게 됩니다.

implications here. First, you should make such effort that even the rafters shake, and second, don't lose sight of the larger goal.

Questioner 2: Thank you, I'll keep working hard.

Kun Sunim: I truly appreciate your efforts. If your legs become strong and you can walk uprightly through this world, what could be better?

Questioner 3 (Male): Hello, I'm a psychiatrist, and a member of the Seon center's science group. I'd like to ask you about how to treat mental illnesses, and schizophrenia in particular.

Among the severe disorders, schizophrenia affects the most people and is one of the most difficult to treat. It's usually what people are seeing when they encounter a "crazy" person, and it affects about one percent of the population. Patients can suffer from auditory and visual hallucinations, and the onset can be sudden or gradual. It completely disrupts their lives, and as it progresses, it often leaves them unable to function in society.

저는 서양의학을 한 사람인데요, 증상은 좀 알려져 있지만 아직 원인이 확실치 않은 이 병의 처방은 주로 약물치료입니다. 약을 평생 먹든가 또는 몇 년 정도 먹게 하면서 치료를 하는데 일단 약을 먹게 되면 환자가 굉장히 멍해지고 정신없어하고 부작용도 굉장히 많습니다.

사실 십 년 이십 년 장기적으로 약을 먹게 되면 의욕도 없어지게 되는 것 같고 자기 주어진 역할도 잘 못하는 그런 사람이 돼 가는 것 같은데 현재로선 이게 가장 좋은 방법이라고 해서 이런 약 처방을 합니다. 환자들에게 "약을 먹어라. 먹어야 한다." 이렇게 말하지만, 부작용 때문에 사실 저 자신도 확신이 없을 때가 많이 있습니다.

이게 최선의 방책인지 이 사람을 위해서 어떻게 해 주는 것이 최선인지 이런 부분에서 늘 갈등을 해 왔었는데 이번 기회에 정신분열을 앓고 있는 대다수의 사람들과 이 병을 치료하고 있는 의사를 대표해서 스님께 한번 여쭤 보고 싶어서 이 자리에 나왔습니다.

대답을 좀 부탁드리겠습니다.

Although doctors know about the symptoms in detail, we have only guesses as to its causes. There are a couple of different medicines that can treat the symptoms, but patients have to take them for the rest of their lives, and they can cause extreme mental fuzziness, and any number of other very unpleasant side effects.

When patients take these for ten or twenty years, they start losing interest in the world around them, almost as if they are losing their desire to live, and have a hard time handling the basics of daily life.

As a doctor, I know that these medicines are the only thing that seems to help this disease, and so I prescribe them and urge my patients to take them. But I myself am uneasy about these drugs.

As a doctor, I've agonized over this for many years, wondering what the best course might be, and if there isn't a better way to treat patients with schizophrenia. I would like to ask you for anything that I and my fellow doctors can use to help people suffering from this disease.

큰스님: 이런 병은 자기한테서 일어나는 것도 있고, 타의에서 들어오는 것도 있고, 조상으로부터 유전되어 받을 수도 있습니다.

그런데 의사들이 볼 때는 증상이 다 똑같다 보니 모두에게 약물을 먹이게 되고, 그러면 낫는 게 아니라 되레 나빠지는 결과가 오게 되죠. 그러니까 의사든 환자든 약물에만 의존할 게 아니라 부모나 가족들, 의사 할 거 없이 주위 사람들이 이 마음공부를 해서 한마음이 되도록 항상 마음을 모아 준다면, 이렇게 환자의 마음에 주입을 한다면, 보이지 않는 데서 작용이 되어 그 병은 생각보다 쉽게 나을 수 있다고 봅니다.

심한 경우 입원을 시켜 치료를 해야 하는 경우도 마찬가지입니다. 그런데 그렇지 않고 자꾸 약물만 투입을 한다면 그 사람은 점차적으로 몸을 버리게 되겠지요. 그러면 삶을 잃고, 용기를 잃고, 의욕을 잃고, 아예 생각하는 것조차 모르게 됩니다. 몸이 살아 있으니까 그냥 움죽거릴 뿐이지요. 사람이 그렇게 된다면 아니 생긴 것만도 못하지 않습니까?

Kun Sunim: This kind of disease can arise from three possible directions. It could be caused by something about the patients themselves, it could be caused by an outside influence, or it could be the results of something their ancestors did.

But to doctors, the symptoms all look the same, so they try to treat each patient in the same way. They give all their patients the same medicine, but it only works for some patients, while causing even more problems for other patients. Thus, doctors and patients need to look beyond just those medicines. The patient's parents, family, and those around them, to say nothing of their doctors, should learn about how to rely upon this fundamental mind.

If they are all working on connecting with this, if they are all inputting the intention that the patient should recover and be able to function and think clearly, then the energy of that will help the patient, who then may be able to recover much easier than expected. When thoroughly entrusted, those intentions can function at the unseen level, where all beings are connected.

그러니 약을 자꾸 먹여 마음을 죽이지 말고 오히려 이 마음을 북돋아 준다면, 그래서 자기 마음에 의해서 육신이 움죽거리는 걸 알게 되면 병이 낫는 거죠. 혹시 여러분이 아는 분 중에 이런 병을 앓고 있는 분이 계신다면 그렇게 관(觀)[16]해 주세요.

이번에 미국에 갔을 때 시카고에 들렀었는데 거기서 아주 흉악한 범죄자들만 있는 교도소를 방문했었어요. 그랬는데 범죄도 범죄지만 머리에 분열증 같은 게 있는 범죄자들을 모아 놓은 큰 방이 있다고 하더군요. 그냥 횡설수설하고 난동을 부리니까 철창에다가 아주 가둬 놓은 거죠. 그래서 그 관리인더러 이렇게 말을 했어요. 그 방 벽에 큰 글씨로 "주인공, 너만이 낫게 할 수 있어."라고 써서 붙이라고요. 그리고 나는 거기다 선신 몇 분만 해 놓고 왔습니다. 손 없는 손이 그네들을 보살펴 준다면 아마 지금은 반 이상 좋아졌을 거라고 믿습니다.

---

16. 관(觀): 어의적으로 '관찰하다' '보다'라는 뜻을 가지고 있으며, 마음공부를 하는 과정에서는 '참나'인 주인공을 믿고 맡기는 것을 뜻함. 즉, 삶에서 부딪치는 모든 문제들을 주인공만이 해결할 수 있다는 철저한 믿음으로 주인공에게 맡겨 놓고 분별없이 집착없이 지켜보는 것을 통틀어 '관'이라 함.

In cases where the schizophrenia is quite severe, you may have to also hospitalize those patients, but everything I just said still applies.

However, if people don't know about this, and just keep giving the patient drugs, then over time their body functions will begin to deteriorate. They begin to lose their vividness, their courage, and their will to live. Finally, even thinking becomes difficult. Their body still lives, so they move about, but what kind of life is this? What's happened to all of the potential they were born with?

So, try to avoid long term use of medicines that will cause their minds to deteriorate. Instead, give them courage, let them know that it is their mind, their foundation that moves and takes care of their body. If they can know this, and begin to trust it, then their illness will start to fade. [To the audience:] Everyone, if you know someone who's suffering from this type of mental illness, raise and entrust this same intention on their behalf.

Recently, I visited a prison in Chicago that housed the most violent offenders. They had a large room where they kept prisoners with severe mental illness, who were too disruptive for the

그러니 의사 선생님도 한번 그렇게 해 보세요. 당신이 그런 분야에 있다니까 하는 말이에요.

질문자 3: 열심히 노력해 보겠습니다.

질문자 4(여): 스님, 저는 질문한다기보다 스님께 고맙다는 인사를 드리러 왔습니다. 제가 여러가지로 마음을 못 잡아서 헤매고 있을 때, 이종 언니가 『무(無)』와 『도(道)』 책을 권해 줘서 읽었습니다. 읽고 나서 내 마음을 한번 들여다봤지요. 진짜 내 마음은 찾지를 못했어요. 그 마음을 찾자니 습(習)[17]을 제거해야 되겠고, 습을 제거하자니 나 자신을 버려야 되겠더라고요. 그런데 그게 참 잘 안되었어요.

---

17. 습(習): 현재뿐만 아니라 과거 수 억겁 년 동안 행하였던 모든 행위들(말, 행동, 생각 등)이 버릇이 되어 잠재여력으로 남아 있는 것을 말함.

regular prison. I asked the person in charge to put a large sign on the wall, saying "Hey! True self! You're the one that can take care of this!" In addition I stationed several good spirits there to help them. With those invisible hands helping, about half the people there should become better. So, since patients like this are your specialty as well, why don't you give this a try! [Smiles.]

Questioner 3: Okay, I'll work hard at doing you've said.

Questioner 4 (female): I came here today to express my deep appreciation for your teachings. I'd been going through a rough time, struggling with despair and confusion, when a cousin gave me your books *Mu* (Nothing) and *Do* (The Path). As I read them, I began to sense something deeper, but although I wanted to find this true mind, I couldn't. I began to realize that I needed to let go of the persistent thoughts of "I" and "me," but I couldn't seem to make much progress with this.

The Doctor is In 125

이번 1월 3일 큰스님을 처음 뵌 날에도 뵙고 나면 좀 잘될 줄 알았지요. 하지만 여전히 그게 잘 안되더군요. 그리고 그냥 그렇게 지냈는데 추석쯤에 갑자기 손이 아파 왔습니다. 그래서 이거를 주인공한테 한번 맡겨 보았지요. 그런데 잘 낫지를 않아 병원엘 갔습니다. 아무리 치료를 해도 안 낫더니 결국 이게 골수암까지 갔습니다. 이것저것 치료가 잘 듣지를 않자 의사 선생님이 뼈 검사를 더 해 보자고 그랬어요.

그때부터 제가 '아니다. 손가락을 끊어 내는 한이 있더라도 두 번 다시 병원에는 안 가고 내 주인공한테 맡기겠다.' 그러면서 한 보름을 견뎌봤어요.

그러고 있는데 그때 큰스님께서 부산 KBS홀에 설법하러 오셔서 부산지원에서 스님을 뵈었지요. '이제는 완전히 손이 낫겠구나.' 하는 생각이 들면서 마음이 완전히 놓였습니다. 그러고 스님 뵙는 순간 몸에 전기가, 전류가 흐름을 느꼈습니다. 며칠

I began to think that it would help if I could meet you in person, and so I came to see you about a year ago. Although it was wonderful, my behavior didn't really change.

I just kept living as I had been until about six months later, when my hand suddenly started hurting. I decided to try entrusting that to my foundation, but it kept bothering me, so I finally went to see a doctor. Nothing they tried seemed to help, and I was finally diagnosed with bone marrow cancer. The doctor used several treatments, but my body didn't respond to any of them. Finally, he wanted to retest me for everything.

At that moment, I wanted nothing more than to completely rely upon my foundation. No more would I go to the hospital looking for hope. I just stayed home, enduring the pain. About two weeks went by like this, when I saw that you were having a large, public Dharma talk in Busan.

I went to the Busan Hanmaum Seon Center to see you, and as I waited, the thought arose, "Ah! Now my hand is going to be completely fine!" As soon as I had that thought, I was able to completely let go of all my fears and worries. And the moment

후에 손이 약간 곪더라고요. 그래서 고름을 내 손으로 직접 짜냈습니다. 짜내고 또 한 며칠 있으니까 아픈 게 완전히 나았어요. 의사 선생님은 사진 안 찍어 보고 검사 안 해 본다고 뭐라 하지만 저는 지금 믿습니다. 지금 아물었어요. 감사합니다.

큰스님: 여러분이 못났든 잘났든 믿는 마음의 능력이란 건 태산을 지고도 남음이 있고 이 우주를 뚫을 수도 있고, 탱크를 부술 수도 있습니다. 이게 어마어마한 도리입니다.

그런 건데 믿지를 못 해 가지고선 그렇게 허우적허우적거리니 사는 게 얼마나 힘들겠습니까? 허공을 허우적거리고 있는 거니까요. 단단히 자기 마음을 믿어서 이 중세계의 통 속에서 세세생생 벗어나십시오.

I did see you, it felt like electricity was flowing through my body. A few days later, a boil appeared on my hand, and I ended up squeezing a lot of pus from it. It healed completely after a few days, and the pain has completely vanished. My doctor wanted me to have more tests and treatments, but I know my hand is fine. Thank you so much.

Kun Sunim: Regardless of who you are, regardless of your position in society, education, gender, or age, every one of you has this incredible fundamental mind within you. If you just have faith in it, and rely upon it, you can move mountains, penetrate the secrets of the universe, and stop army tanks in their tracks.

But if you don't have faith in it, if you try to ignore it, then life is like trying to walk through an endless field of mud. Or floundering through the air, unable to get your feet under you. Please work on firmly trusting this inherent foundation of yours, so that you will be able to step beyond the boundaries of this middle world and become forever free.

틀림없이 여기서만이, 여기 내 마음에서만이 할 수 있다는 믿음! (주먹을 쥐어 보이시며) 이것이야말로 바로 이 세상을 딱 뒤집어 놓고, 또 바로 세울 수도 있는 그런 용기와 패기가 생기게 하는 겁니다. 또 질문하실 게 있으면 하세요. 없습니까?

우리가 지금 한 다리 절름발이고요, 한쪽 눈 장님이고요, 한쪽 귀 귀머거리예요. 아까도 얘기를 했지만 레이저 광선과 같은 첨단 기술이 지금 세계적으로 없어서는 안 되는 존재지만 이 마음의 심력(心力)만은 못하다 이겁니다. 이런 기술들은 반밖엔 그 역할을 못하니까요.

그러니 내가 더 높으니 네가 더 높으니 이러지 말고 한 도반으로서 이 공부를 열심히 해야 우리 모두가 진정으로 더 나은 삶을 살 수가 있어요. 부처님께서는 모두가 자기 아님이 없기 때문에 어느 누구라도 똥 누면 밑을 씻어 줘 가면서 보살펴 주십니다.

Know that this inherent mind can take care of whatever you are going through! Believe in your inherent essence! [Thrusting her fist in the air.] This is where you can find courage! And vision and determination! Here is the power to turn the world upside down or to set it right!

Right now we are lame in one leg, blind in one eye, and deaf in one ear. Even the most advanced technology in the world, like lasers and such, can't compare to this ability of your inherent essence. Why? Because those are limited to the material world, to only one side of things. But this light within you is connected to both sides, as well as all the energy of the universe.

So leave behind thoughts of social status or judgements about others, and work together as brothers and sisters in the Dharma. The Buddha awakened to the reality that everyone else was also himself, so even cleaning someone else's bottom after a bowel movement was no more than cleaning his own. Should even a dog, sick with disease, raise from its foundation a deep desire for help, Buddha transforms into a dog and helps cure

하다못해 개가 염원을 해도 개로 화(化)해서 병을 고쳐 주시고 또 무명(無明)[18]을 벗겨 주십니다. 이렇게 하시는 것을 어떠한 사람의 이름이 아니라, 한 개체로서가 아니라, 이 천체 한 덩어리(손가락을 하나 세워 보이시고)의 한 불기둥을 이름해서 그걸 부처라고 한 겁니다.

다시 말해, 우리의 이 체가 없는 마음의 작용을 일컬어 '도리천'이라 하는데, 이는 천체 한 기둥을 말합니다. 그러니까 한 기둥의 마음으로서, 우리가 심력을 똑바로 길러서 애고라든가 병고라든가, 어떠한 업식이라도 다 그냥 태워 버립시다.

---

18. 무명(無明, *avidya*): 진리에 통달하지 못해 밝지 못한 마음의 상태. 무지(無知), 어리석음, 지혜가 없음을 뜻하며, 이로 인해 진리를 바로 볼 수 없게 되고, 생로병사(生老病死)에서 비롯되는 모든 고통과 번뇌의 근원이 됨.

the disease, or frees the dog from its ignorance.[23] Here, "Buddha" does not refer to an individual, but rather to the great pillar of energy that is the whole.

Every single one of us has this incredible, formless mind, this one great pillar that encompasses everything, which the ancients called the "Highest Heaven of Mt. Sumeru." Take this pillar as your center, and strengthen your ability to let go. Develop your ability to entrust it with everything. In this way, let's take all suffering, all illness, every kind of karmic state of consciousness, and burn it all up!

---

23. In this case, ignorance means the unenlightened habits that caused that dog to be born as a dog, thus, "freeing it from its ignorance" can mean helping the dog so it can move forward and grow, or it can even mean helping it to peacefully leave its body and then helping it to be reborn in better circumstances or at a higher level of existence.

한마음출판사의 마음을 밝혀 주는 도서

- A Thousand Hands of Compassion
  만가지 꽃이 피고 만가지 열매 익어
  : 대행큰스님의 뜻으로 푼 천수경 (한글/영어)
  [2010 iF Communication Design Award 수상]
- Wake Up And Laugh (영어)
- No River To Cross, No Raft To Find (영어)
- Standing Again (영어)
- It's Hard To Say (영어) (절판)
- My Heart Is A Golden Buddha (영어, 오디오북)
- One Mind: Principles (영어)
- Touching The Earth (영어)
- Sharing The Same Heart (영어)
- 생활 속의 참선수행 (시리즈) (한글/영어)
  1. 죽어야 나를 보리라
     (To Discover Your True Self, "I" Must Die)
  2. 함이 없이 하는 도리 (Walking Without A Trace)
  3. 맡겨놓고 지켜봐라 (Let Go And Observe)
  4. 마음은 보이지 않는 행복의 창고
     (Mind, Treasure House Of Happiness)
  5. 일체를 용광로에 넣어라
     (The Furnace Within Yourself)
  6. 온 우주를 살리는 마음의 불씨
     (The Spark That Can Save The Universe)
  7. 한마음의 위력
     (The Infinite Power Of One Mind)
  8. 일체를 움직이는 그 자리
     (In The Heart Of A Moment)

9. 한마음 한뜻이 되어 (One With The Universe)
  10. 지구보존 (Protecting The Earth)
  11. 진짜 통하게 되면 (Inherent Connections)
  12. 잘 돼야 돼! (Finding A Way Forward)
  13. 믿는 만큼 行한 만큼 (Faith In Action)
  14. 병을 고치는 최고의 방법
  　　(The Healing Power of Our Inner Light)
  15. 내 안에 의사가 있다구요?! (The Doctor Is In)
- 내 마음은 금부처 (한글 - CD 포함)
- 건널 강이 어디 있으랴 (한글)
- 처음 시작하는 마음공부1 (한글)
- Grundlagen (독일어, 2018 New)
- El Camino Interior (스페인어)
- Vida De La Maestra Seon Daehaeng (스페인어)
- Enseñanzas De La Maestra Daehaeng (스페인어)
- Práctica Del Seon En La Vida Diaria (Colección) (스페인어/영어)
  1. Una Semilla Inherente Alimenta El Universo
     (The Spark That Can Save The Universe)
- Si Te Lo Propones, No Hay Imposibles (스페인어)
- 人生不是苦海 (번체자 중국어) (개정판)
- 无河可渡 (간체자 중국어)
- 我心是金佛 (간체자 중국어) (개정판)

해외출판사에서 출판된 한마음도서

- Wake Up And Laugh
  Wisdom Publications, 미국

- No River To Cross
  (*No River To Cross, No Raft To Find* 영어판)
  Wisdom Publications, 미국

- Wie Fließendes Wasser
  (*My Heart Is A Golden Buddha* 독일어판)
  Goldmann Arkana-Random House, 독일

- Wie Fließendes Wasser - CD
  (*My Heart Is A Golden Buddha* 독일어판 오디오북)
  steinbach sprechende bücher

- Ningún Río Que Cruzar
  (*No River To Cross* 스페인어판)
  Kailas Editorial, S.L., 스페인

- Umarmt Von Mitgefühl
  ('만가지 꽃이 피고 만가지 열매 익어':
  대행큰스님의 뜻으로 푼 천수경 독일어판)
  Diederichs-Random House, 독일

- 我心是金佛
  (*My Heart Is A Golden Buddha* 번체자 중국어판)
  橡樹林文化出版, 대만

- Vertraue Und Lass Alles Los
  (*No River To Cross* 독일어판)
  Goldmann Arkana-Random House, 독일

- Wache Auf Und Lache
  (*Wake Up And Laugh* 독일어판)
  Theseus, 독일

- Дзэн И Просветление
  (*No River To Cross* 러시아어판)
  Amrita-Rus, 러시아

- Sup Cacing Tanah
  (*My Heart Is A Golden Buddha* 인도네시아어판)
  PT Gramedia, 인도네시아

- Không có sông nào để vượt qua
  (*No River To Cross* 베트남어판)
  Vien Chieu, 베트남

- Probuď se!
  (*Wake Up And Laugh* 체코어판)
  (Eugenika, 체코)

- tỉnh thức và cười
  (*Wake Up And Laugh* 베트남어판)
  Vien Chieu, 베트남

Other Books by Seon Master Daehaeng

English
- Wake Up And Laugh (Wisdom Publications)
- No River To Cross (Wisdom Publications)
- My Heart Is A Golden Buddha (Hanmaum Publications)
  Also available as an audiobook
- Standing Again (Hanmaum Publications)
- Sharing the Same Heart (Hanmaum Publications)
- Touching The Earth (Hanmaum Publications)
- A Thousand Hands of Compassion
  (Hanmaum Publications) [Korean/English]
- One Mind: Principles (Hanmaum Publications)
  All of these are available in paper or ebook formats

- Practice in Daily Life (Korean/English bilingual series)
  1. To Discover Your True Self, "I" Must Die
  2. Walking Without A Trace
  3. Let Go And Observe
  4. Mind, Treasure House Of Happiness
  5. The Furnace Within Yourself
  6. The Spark That Can Save The Universe
  7. The Infinite Power Of One Mind
  8. In The Heart of A Moment
  9. One With The Universe
  10. Protecting The Earth
  11. Inherent Connections
  12. Finding A Way Forward
  13. Faith In Action
  14. The Healing Power of Our Inner Light
  15. The Doctor Is In (New)
  16. Dissolving Our Karma (Forthcoming)

Korean
- 건널 강이 어디 있으랴 (Hanmaum Publications)
- 내 마음은 금부처 (Hanmaum Publications)
- 처음 시작하는 마음공부1 (Hanmaum Publications)

Russian
- Дзэн И Просветление (Amrita-Rus)

German
- Wache Auf und Lache (Theseus)
- Umarmt von Mitgefühl (Deutsch·Koreanisch, Diederichs)
- Wie fließendes Wasser (Goldmann)
- Wie fließendes Wasser - CD (steinbach sprechende bücher)
- Vertraue und lass alles los (Goldmann)
- Grundlagen (Hanmaum Publications, New)

Czech
- Probuď se! (Eugenika)

Spanish
- Ningún Río Que Cruzar (Kailas Editorial)
- Una Semilla Inherente Alimenta El Universo (Hanmaum Publications)
- Si Te Lo Propones, No Hay Imposibles (Hanmaum Publications)
- El Camino Interior (Hanmaum Publications)
- Vida De La Maestra Seon Daehaeng (Hanmaum Publications)
- Enseñanzas De La Maestra Daehaeng (Hanmaum Publications)

Indonesian
- Sup Cacing Tanah (PT Gramedia)

Vietnamese
- Không có sông nào để vượt qua (Hanmaum Publications; Vien Chieu, Vietnam)
- tỉnh thức và cười (Hanmaum Publications; Vien Chieu, Vietnam)

Chinese
- 我心是金佛（简体字）(Hanmaum Publications, 韩国)
- 无河可渡（简体字）(Hanmaum Publications, 韩国)
- 人生不是苦海（繁体字）(Hanmaum Publications, 韩国)
- 我心是金佛（繁体字）(橡树林文化出版，台湾)

한마음선원본원

경기도 안양시 만안구 경수대로 1282 (석수동, 한마음선원)
(우) 13908

Tel : 82-31-470-3100 Fax : 82-31-470-3116
홈페이지 : http://www.hanmaum.org
이메일 : jongmuso@hanmaum.org

국내지원

강릉지원 (우)25565 강원도 강릉시 하평5길 29 (포남동)
　　　　　TEL:(033) 651-3003   FAX:(033) 652-0281

공주지원 (우)32522 충청남도 공주시 사곡면 위안양골길 157-61
　　　　　TEL:(041) 852-9100   FAX:(041) 852-9105

광명선원 (우)27638 충청북도 음성군 금왕읍 대금로 1402
　　　　　TEL:(043) 877-5000   FAX:(043) 877-2900

광주지원 (우)61965 광주광역시 서구 운천로 204번길 23-1 (치평동)
　　　　　TEL:(062) 373-8801   FAX:(062) 373-0174

대구지원 (우)42152 대구광역시 수성구 수성로 41길 76 (중동)
　　　　　TEL:(053) 767-3100   FAX:(053) 765-1600

목포지원 (우)58696 전라남도 목포시 백년대로 266번길 31-1 (상동)
　　　　　TEL:(061) 284-1771   FAX:(061) 284-1770

문경지원 (우)36937 경상북도 문경시 산양면 봉서1길 10
　　　　　TEL:(054) 555-8871   FAX:(054) 556-1989

부산지원 (우)49113 부산광역시 영도구 함지로 79번길 23-26 (동삼동)
　　　　　TEL:(051) 403-7077   FAX:(051) 403-1077

울산지원 (우)44200 울산광역시 북구 달래골길 26-12 (천곡동)
　　　　　TEL:(052) 295-2335   FAX:(052) 295-2336

제주지원 (우)63308 제주특별자치도 제주시 황사평6길 176-1 (영평동)
TEL:(064) 727-3100   FAX:(064) 727-0302

중부경남 (우)50871 경상남도 김해시 진영읍 하계로35
TEL:(055) 345-9900   FAX:(055) 346-2179

진주지원 (우)52602 경상남도 진주시 미천면 오방로 528-40
TEL:(055) 746-8163   FAX:(055) 746-7825

청주지원 (우)28540 충청북도 청주시 청원구 교서로 109
TEL:(043) 259-5599   FAX:(043) 255-5599

통영지원 (우)53021 경상남도 통영시 광도면 조암길 45-230
TEL:(055) 643-0643   FAX:(055) 643-0642

포항지원 (우)37635 경상북도 포항시 북구 우창로 59 (우현동)
TEL:(054) 232-3163   FAX:(054) 241-3503

Anyang Headquarters of Hanmaum Seonwon

1282 Gyeongsu-daero, Manan-gu, Anyang-si,
Gyeonggi-do, 13908, Republic of Korea
Tel: (82-31) 470-3175 / Fax: (82-31) 470-3209
www.hanmaum.org/eng
onemind@hanmaum.org

Overseas Branches of Hanmaum Seonwon

ARGENTINA
Buenos Aires
Miró 1575, CABA, C1406CVE, Rep. Argentina
Tel: (54-11) 4921-9286 / Fax: (54-11) 4921-9286
http://hanmaumbsas.org

Tucumán
Av. Aconquija 5250, El Corte, Yerba Buena,
Tucumán, T4107CHN, Rep. Argentina
Tel: (54-381) 425-1400
www.hanmaumtuc.org

BRASIL
São Paulo
R. Newton Prado 540, Bom Retiro
Sao Paulo, CEP 01127-000, Brasil
Tel: (55-11) 3337-5291
www.hanmaumbr.org

CANADA
Toronto
20 Mobile Dr., North York, Ontario M4A 1H9, Canada
Tel: (1-416) 750-7943
www.hanmaum.org/toronto

GERMANY
Kaarst
Broicherdorf Str. 102, 41564 Kaarst, Germany
Tel: (49-2131) 969551 / Fax: (49-2131) 969552
www.hanmaum-zen.de

THAILAND
Bangkok
86/1 Soi 4 Ekamai Sukhumvit 63
Bangkok, Thailand
Tel: (66-2) 391-0091
www.hanmaum.org/cafe/thaihanmaum

USA
Chicago
7852 N. Lincoln Ave., Skokie, IL 60077, USA
Tel: (1-847) 674-0811
www.hanmaum.org/chicago

Los Angeles
1905 S. Victoria Ave., L.A., CA 90016, USA
Tel: (1-323) 766-1316
www.hanmaum.org/la

New York
144-39, 32 Ave., Flushing, NY 11354, USA
Tel: (1-718) 460-2019 / Fax: (1-718) 939-3974
www.juingong.org

Washington D.C.
7807 Trammel Rd., Annandale, VA 22003, USA
Tel: (1-703) 560-5166
www.hanmaum.org/wa

책에 관한 문의나 주문을 하실 분들은
아래의 연락처로 문의해 주십시오.

한마음국제문화원/한마음출판사
경기도 안양시 만안구 경수대로 1282 (우)13908
전화: (82-31) 470-3175
팩스: (82-31) 470-3209
e-mail: onemind@hanmaum.org
hanmaumbooks.org

If you would like more information about these
books or would like to order copies of them,
please call or write to:

Hanmaum International Culture Institute
Hanmaum Publications
1282 Gyeongsu-daero, Manan-gu, Anyang-si,
Gyeonggi-do, 13908,
Republic of Korea
Tel: (82-31) 470-3175
Fax: (82-31) 470-3209
e-mail: onemind@hanmaum.org
hanmaumbooks.org